Tomoya Masuda
Henri Stierlin (Ed.)

Japan

Photos: Yukio Futagawa

Benedikt Taschen

Editor of Series	Henri Stierlin
Plans	Tomoya Masuda, Tokyo, and Jean Duret, Geneva
English Editor	Ron Toby

Contents

Modern Architecture and Japanese Tradition

First of all, Japan produced works of 'Japanese' style. Later on, her approach to building revealed various exemplary trends, whose interpretation is probably based on a misunderstanding.

Indeed, since modern architecture has existed, the traditional Japanese house has appeared striking in its 'modernity'. The Europeans used it first as a source of plastic design; to the flat effects of the Impressionists corresponded, a quarter of a century later, that refinement in the division and distribution of pure surfaces that is so typical of architects who are devotees of rationalism. It was not long before these architects discovered, behind the geometrical and graphic characteristics, the principles of modular composition and the high degree of standardization in a system which goes far beyond the point of mere ingenuity.

Bruno Taut admired the 'cleanness' of these architectonic products. In Japan's past, references were found by those who speculated on pure volumes, the abolition of ornament and the reduction of architecture to a combination of planes, implying the idea of an assembly of simple elements. 'It is the fact of enclosing that is significant, not the space enclosed' (Noguchi).

For this evolution to take place, attention had had to be shifted from the complicated, ornate Buddhist temples to buildings more in keeping with our own sensibility, like the Ise shrines and the Katsura palace. Different as they were in age and purpose, those edifices also revealed a process which appeared essential to the structuralists: Mies van der Rohe, who never went to Japan, regarded Japanese architecture as the perfect expression of a method based on an absolute distinction between the envelope and the framework, to such an extent that it could be reduced, as in his own American works, to an ideal equation: architecture = rational structure.

To these very dissimilar interpretations, we must add at least a third, which is in fact earlier and lays stress on quite different qualities. The sense of spatial values which is such a feature of so-called organic architecture enabled Wright, early in the century, to identify other components as well. In his view, the simplification process from which Japanese architecture had developed seemed to have exerted its influence less on actual form and construction than through the 'elimination of the insignificant'. The extreme demand for quality which is evidenced in the Shinjuan monastery or in the Golden Pavilion at Kyōto, as in the humblest farm, is manifest in a constant concern for the human scale and an unfailing respect for the materials used, according to their nature. Above all, however, the architects of the organic movement admired the extensibility of the buildings and the permanent exchange established in them between 'inside' and 'outside'.

Imperial Villa, Katsura

1 main gateway
2 entrance
3 Gepparo tea pavilion
4 verandah
5 'ko-shoin' (the oldest part)
6 'chu-shoin' (middle shoin)
7 'shin-shoin' (the new shoin)
8 verandah
9 moss
10 lawn

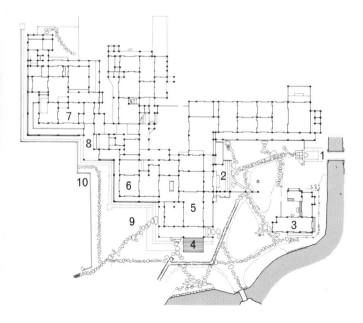

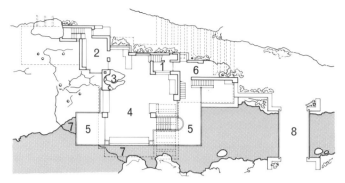

Plan of Falling Water villa, by Frank Lloyd Wright

| 1 entrance | 3 fireplace | 5 terrace | 7 waterfall |
| 2 kitchen | 4 living-room | 6 loggia | 8 bridge |

The palace at Katsura, the supreme example, justified all the theories. Its way of standing out against its surroundings and 'activating' the landscape, its piles, the texture of its composition and its sliding panels made it a sort of Villa Savoye (Le Corbusier, 1928) before its time. But its spaced posts, the analytic incorporation of its constructional elements and its Mondrian-like walls suggested a parallel with the Illinois Technological Institute (Mies van der Rohe, 1938). Its free plan, the insistence of its broad roofs (which the rationalists had mentally wiped out), the protective screens–not fragments of infinite planes intersecting at right-angles, but light protections from wind, rain and sun–and the integration of the building into the site by means of successive volumes and unfinished materials, as well as the contrast between the basic grid and the highly 'spontaneous' appendages attached to it: all this prefigured the poetic manner of Wright, from the Prairie Houses 1900–14) to the Falling Water villa (1936).

In brief, the more diversified the tendencies of western architecture become, the more affinities they find with the architecture of Japan. Certain questions might already have been added to those mentioned above: when the Bauhaus and the CIAM raise the problem of the minimum dwelling, they start from the hypothesis that living-accommodation is not a matter of class, but of organization; in Japan, however, the Emperor lives in the same way as the peasant, for it is not the way of life that distinguishes the one from the other. And when western architecture seeks to recuperate the tactile values which its puritanical phase has put into hibernation for some time to come, there is no doubt (for example) that the differentiation of floor surfaces by the texture of the material felt by the foot, which is typical of Japanese tradition, will provide new retrospective models.

Confronted as it is with the most varied western conceptions, Japanese architecture is unique among the exotic forms of the art in so far as it always responds in an appropriate manner. This ability identifies it with a symbol which is exhausted by no single interpretation, for each one is superimposed upon its predecessors without in any way excluding them: Japan justifies every tendency. It lay with Gropius, with his fundamental eclecticism, to include them all in his preface to a work on Katsura.

It must be mentioned, nevertheless, that if modern architects have been struck by those aspects that are most in keeping with their own research, it is because this architecture was capable of receiving their projections. Borrowing at first only some elements of writing, the West has ultimately discovered a syntax and an idiom: surfaces, modules, volumes, structures, space, flooring and the total environment – Japan had invented the entire system and defined the course now followed by western research on the essence of the architectural phenomenon.

But it is high time to add that this enthusiasm of the West, due to the tuning of our own creative and critical processes, has never been impelled, to quote Francastel, by the desire to approach the state of mind that inspired the works which have been discovered. The Japanese idea of Japanese architecture has remained foreign to us; the schematic means whereby we have grasped the significance of that architecture have nothing to do with the Japanese mentality.

Since the end of the nineteenth century, as a matter of fact, Japanese tradition and western research have differed in every respect, in their causes and their notions alike. Japanese architecture comes into being under a feudal regime, in a damp climate; it makes use of perishable and replaceable materials, which have to be light in weight on account of the earthquakes. Neither its creators nor its users belong to a humanistic civilization; they know nothing of individualism; they live in a cyclic time system; they have not been through the trials of linear perspective or the cubist revolution. In its relationship with nature, Japanese architecture seeks simultaneously to attain ends which are treated antithetically by western architects and which even serve to distinguish them: the window is a frame for 'natural pictures' in Japan, as with Neutra or Rietveld, but the garden forms a continuous unity with the house, as with Wright or Aalto.

But the thing that strikes the westerner most is that the very word 'architecture' is inexistent in Japanese tradition. There is 'zoka', which concerns the construction of houses, and 'fushin', which concerns the collection of funds for the building or rebuilding of temples; these are not abstract terms, but words denoting precise acts, as in mediaeval Christendom. The word 'kenchiku', recently invented by men of letters to denote the general reality that we call architecture is used in practice for all building operations collectively. And to have quality, architecture must be 'shibui' – an adjective covering six or seven qualifications, each one accompanied by a corrective... (Quiet, but not inert; beautiful, but not superficial; simple, but without ostentation; sober, but interesting and vital; original, but familiar; stable and indigenous, as opposed to the ephemeral character of fashion.)

Are we to conclude that the 'reading' worked out by our western architects was a mere simulation? It has no doubt been understood that the wealth of a reality is not measured only by the exactitude of its outlines, but also by the limits which are assigned to it and tolerated by it.

André Corboz,
Professor of the School of
Architecture of Montreal
University

Introduction

In 1636, eighty-seven years after Francisco de Xavier set up his first Jesuit mission in Kagoshima, at the southern end of Kyūshū, and 232 years before the restoration of Imperial rule, the Tokugawa Government decided on a policy of exclusion of foreign influences, and, as a result, Japan closed her ports to the world. The decision, which was taken more for political than religious reasons, resulted in the complete isolation of Japan from the intellectual and scientific achievements of contemporary Europe, and the effects on her culture were far reaching. Like a pearl slowly growing inside the shell of an oyster, Japanese-ness, or the Japanese mentality, the unique way of thinking and feeling which had evolved over 5,000 years, continued to develop and preserve its traditions almost to the end of the nineteenth century.

The seclusion policy was feasible only because Japan is composed of a number of islands. The Japanese archipelago faces the Pacific Ocean and the eastern edge of the Eurasian continent. It is composed of four main islands: Hokkaidō, Honshū, Shikoku and Kyūshū, and a chain of more than 1,000 smaller ones that stretch for some 800 miles from north to south. These constitute the main part of the Festoon Archipelago of the West Pacific, together with the Kuriles to the north-east, and the Ryūkyūs in the south-west. Crossing the arc of Japan nearly at its centre is the Shichitō-Mariana Island chain which extends southward. The islands of these groups are the tops of mountains some of which reach to a height of more than 30,000 feet above the depths of the sea trenches lying off their eastern coasts.

According to the ancient Japanese legends, two gods gave birth to the eight main islands. Geologically the present islands were isolated from the mainland at the end of the Pleistocene Period, about 20,000 years ago, as a result of repeated movements of the earth's crust which had begun in the Middle Palaeozoic era. The circum-pacific orogenic seismic and volcanic belts lie within and along the Japanese islands, and in Japan the movements of the earth's crust were more peculiar and complex than in other regions. At least four violent orogenic movements took place, the first of which thrust the land above the level of the sea early in the Carboniferous Era.

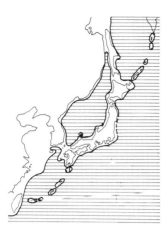

The Japanese islands in the Third Ice Age

Then the belts of the Shichitō-Mariana, the Ezo-Sakhalin, the Ryūkyū, and the Kurile groups were formed.

Geological Movements

During the early Miocene Period there was severe volcanic activity in the southern Fossa Magna, a rupture-zone in central Japan which separated the south-west of Japan geologically (and at one period culturally) from the north-east. One result of this prolonged activity was Mount Fuji. Apart from the main central volcanic belt along the Japanese chain, there are several other volcanic zones, most of which first became active at the beginning of the Pleistocene Era. There are 188 volcanoes in Japan, of which more than 40 are still active. Throughout these periods there were frequent land bridges to East Asia.

Since the beginning of the Pleistocene Era the Japanese islands tended to be thrust upward, and there were frequent changes in topography due to upheavals of the crust combined with volcanic activity, and also to variations of sea level in the Ice Age. The Kantō loam bed, which covers the terraces of the Kantō Plain at altitudes of between ten and sixty metres above sea-level, is said to be an aeolean quaternary deposit of volcanic ash. The loam in its turn is covered by humus soil to a depth of a yard and contains examples of prehistoric earthenwares. The topmost layers of loam contain pre-pottery age stone implements such as axe-blades, knife blades and points, similar to the late Palaeolithic culture of Europe, while the middle layers have yielded finds of handaxes and choppers belonging to the period in Europe when Neanderthal man was replaced by Homo sapiens about 50,000 years ago.

In 1963, Homo sapiens fossils were found in fissure deposits in the central area of Honshū together with many fossils of Upper Pleistocene fauna, including the tusk of a Japanese dwarf variety of the southern elephant Paleoroxodon aomoriensis. But the racial relationship between stone culture inhabitants of Pleistocene Japan and the first Upper Pleistocene hunters who migrated from north-eastern Asia to America toward the end of the Pleistocene Period, about 15,000 to 20,000 years ago, is not clear because we do not yet know if the Tsugaru Strait between Honshū and Hokkaidō was closed at the time. Furthermore, even the relationship between Paleolithic Homo sapiens and the prehistoric Japanese with their earthenware culture, has not yet been clarified. It is worth noting, however, that the fossils of fauna and flora unearthed in Japan are of mixed southern and northern origin. This is a result of the changes in the entrance routes due to frequent reappearance of land bridges to the continent until the end of the Pleistocene Era.

The terrestial movements of the Japanese archipelago have never stopped. The average earthquake frequency in the group is 7,500 per year, and one-fifth of these are perceptible to the human body. 420 major earthquakes have been recorded in one thousand years of Japanese history, often in such magnitudes as to cause sudden and momentous upheavals. In addition to these abrupt changes along the archipelago, there is an undulating vertical land-mass movement of 125–150 miles along the sea-coasts of Japan and the Pacific, as well as a horizontal shearing movement across Honshū along the line between Tsuruga and Ise bays. Thus the topography and the 16,000 mile coastline of Japan are constantly chang-

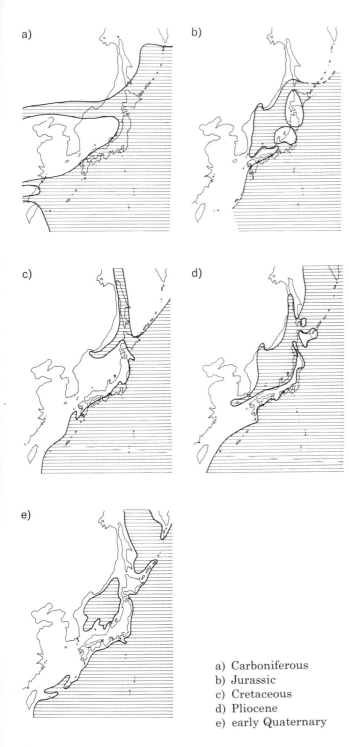

a) Carboniferous
b) Jurassic
c) Cretaceous
d) Pliocene
e) early Quaternary

ing; these permanent terrestial fluctuations most probably have something to do with the acute feeling for change that the Japanese possess.

Because of the violent and complicated movements of the earth's crust which created Japan, the islands are very mountainous; most of the plains and basins, which make up only 24% of the total area, are depressive in origin, and therefore the tectonic by-products of the mountains. Topographically the plains are like small-scale mosaic work, crisscrossed by rivers and full of variety, contrasting with the steep-sided mountains. The process of upheaval and subsidence in mountain and plain is still going on.

The alluvial plains below an altitude of thirty-five feet above sea-level were once under water and gradually emerged about 5,000 years ago. The areas below fifteen feet were, for the most part, artificially constructed in the historic period.

Climate

Factors both global and geographical influence the climate in Japan. The long arcs of the islands extend over twenty degrees of latitude from the subtropical south to the semi-frigid north, forming a border between the largest continent and the largest ocean in the world. Their shores are washed by the warm Japan Current in the south, and by the cold Kurile Current in the north. Thus Japan's climate varies between extremes: subtropical and oceanic in the summer, with warm rain and high humidity, and semi-frigid continental winters, with cold and snow. The islands are poised between the cold, dry air mass of Siberia and the warm, wet air mass of the northern Pacific, and are crossed by both cold and warm fronts, according to the season. This alternation of cold and warm fronts associated with the westerly upper air current creates periods of long and heavy rainfall before and after the summer, which probably accounts for the deep overhang of the eaves of traditional Japanese houses. Again, almost every year, typhoons are born in the extremely low-pressure area north of the Equator. They move at first to the north-west, and then, turning north and north-east at the beginning of autumn, activate a heavy rain belt, which falls on the southern coastal districts of Japan, often causing serious storm, flood, and wind damage.

The Japanese and Nature

These climatic factors produce delicate shifts and variations of the seasons which, together with the unstable and multifarious weather, have contributed greatly to the formation of the Japanese mentality. The symbolic sonnets called 'haiku', expressing the sense of the seasons, would never have been created without such a climatic environment. There are more than twenty words in the Japanese language to describe the different types of rain, according to the seasons or winds. In contrast, there is a scarcity of names for the stars, partly because they are obscured by the rainy sky and partly because of the concentration of the Japanese interest in delicate earthly changes rather than in heavenly permanency. The tendency of the Japanese toward an interest in existentia rather than essentia will be more clearly shown if a comparison is made between the extreme richness of adjectives describing bodily feeling and the meagreness of the names of the parts or the organs of the body itself.

Due to the delicate changes and shifts of the environment the Japanese character is intuitive, emotional, situational, paradoxical and irrational. The agile, responsive person is by nature sensitive to every symptom of change, and the Japanese sensitivity has inevitably and continually developed in the ever-changing climatic circumstances. Thus the ability to grasp intuitively the significance of a situation became the basis from which Japanese symbolism was likely to develop. In the past, in the Japanese language, such a symptom or presentiment was known as 'ke', 'kehai' or 'mono-no-ke'. But more generally 'ke', meaning strangeness and possibly a humour, is a kind of potency, the application of which, 'kehai', is assumed to cause some substantial effect on man. And 'mono', meaning thing or being, possesses and exerts this same potency, or rather, 'mono' may be identified with this potency. Thus 'mono' as a thing or being is no more than a potency expected to be substantial even if 'mono' as the thing itself is physical at the same time. This potency of the thing is a symptom of 'being' in another word. Therefore the sensitivity to every symptom of change is the sensitivity to the potency or the vector of being. This is the real basis of the structure of architectural space in Japan, because only when being, in this case space, is vectorial is the structuralization of it possible.

If being is vectorial, that is to say, symbolic, then sensitivity may be concerned not only with sensation, but also with emotion, however primitive it is. Japanese words describing emotion are extremely delicate and rich, but those describing sensation are few and rather crude. This emotional sensitivity is really the peculiarity of the Japanese mentality, and the symbolism of Japan mainly has to do with emotional meaning, as expressed in such words as 'sabi', 'wabi' or 'iki'. 'Wabi' and 'sabi' refer to the uniquely purified and idealized emotional meaning of the geographical environment or natural landscape, and 'iki', of the social environment, or human relationships. The multifarious spatiotemporal changes of the landscape inevitably led the Japanese to contemplate and pay serious consideration to the environment, as well as to human relations. Thus there are abundant aesthetic and ethical words in Japanese which derive from the environment. Many of these ancient ethical words originally had a spatio-luminous sense, which indicates the deep association of the ancient Japanese mentality with the natural scene, not with what might be termed religious feeling.

Japanese Mentality

The climatic character of Japan, and, naturally, the flora and fauna, are both tropical and frigid, continental, oceanic and seasonal, as well as sudden, in the case of the typhoon. All these features are opposite and paradoxical, but the Japanese have no freedom of choice; the entire environment is given: it is physical fact, and actual. The only possibility of selection' exists between physical actuality and non-physical state, that is to say the imagination. The Japanese very often prefer imagination to fact, and it is one of the essentials of Japanese symbolism, expecially of aesthetic symbolism. Since the Japanese have no choice in their context of living, such European thought modes as 'either-or' dichotomy are alien to them. Japanese may think 'this-and-that' which usually seems paradoxical and ambiguous to the European.

Because of his acceptance of actuality and his submission to it, the Japanese is essentially a realist and a naturalist in his worldly life. By careful, intensive cultivation, he improved his agrarian skills, and adapted his rice to difficult and hostile conditions. In concordance with his peculiar concepts of nature and metamorphosis, he created such magnificent worlds of imagination as the tea ceremony, or Japanese gardening. And curiously enough these metamorphoses did not take place as a linear extension of daily life to the other world after death, but as a parallel to it. The Japanese lived in both the worlds of actuality and of imagination at the same time. This will be clear if we consider the Japanese idea of a house – 'ie'. There are three main interpretations of the generic meaning of the word 'ie': the fireplace, the sleeping place and the vessel; its contemporary meaning as a building 'per se' is of later origin. Later, the concept of 'ie' broadened to include the premises, the family and the lineage of the family, sometimes with a mythical ancestor. It is also interesting to note that such family associations as sons-in-law, and sworn brothers, or henchmen, are also contained in the concept of 'ie'. This entire complex was, in medieval times, inherited by the heir as an estate. Thus the spatial concept of 'ie' may be seen in the importance put on the organic wholeness of the interior rather than on the individual units it comprises.

Ethnical Origin

Paying only scant attention to the practical aspects of everyday life has been peculiar to the Japanese, in the most general use of the word Japanese to cover the whole range of peoples and cultures which have gone to make up the Japanese race.

Of the present human stocks in Japan, four ethnic types can be distinguished: the Tungus, the Mongolian, the Malayan and the Ainu. Each of them mi-grated to the Japanese archipelago by a different route, or at a different time, and have different physiques and physiognomies. The first two ethnic types went through a process of antagonism and fusion in the prehistoric Korean peninsula. According to a recent study of the physique of the contemporary Japanese there are two essential types: the Tohoku in the north-east, and the Kinki in the middle-west. The former resemble the Ainu hybrid in Hokkaidō, the latter, the southern Korean. The geographical distribution of these and intermediate types in modern Japan indicates that Tohoku stock probably migrated to the islands first, followed by the Kinki, who arrived in the midwest via the Inland Sea, and gradually moved further to the east. It is also possible to distinguish influences of two other types of Chinese and other southern stocks, although their exact nature is not yet clear.

The Language

However, the theory proposed by some linguists as to the prehistoric movement of the immigrants is quite the opposite. The ancient Japanese words, 'Yamato kotoba', constitute about 60 per cent of the vocabulary in present daily use, and 30–40 per cent of the vocabulary in the modern dictionary. The others are mostly Japanese borrowings from Chinese, and Japanese coinages borrowing Chinese letters, the 'join-go'. Ancient Japanese is said to have many definite linguistic features common to Polynesian languages, especially phonetically. But there is a greater similarity of words and grammatical construction between ancient Japanese and southern Korean, and some of these common features are of the Ural-Altaic lineage, now partly lost in both languages. Since the most durable feature of a language when it comes in contact with another is said to be the phonetic system, the disappearance of the Ural-Altaic vowel harmony and the persistance of Polynesian phonetics in modern Japanese would indicate that the languages were introduced into Japan at different epochs. Thus in the Neolithic Period the inhabitants of Japan probably spoke a language or languages related to the south-asian linguistic stock, while the northern language group with a Ural-Altaic grammar system and vowel harmony migrated to Japan at a later period.

The Myths

Some mythologists recognize two remarkable stages in the introduction of different groups of myths into Japan which are inconsistent with the linguistic version. In general, it is possible to divide Japanese mythology into four main types according to the plot of the story:

Historic sites in Japan

1 Suwa
2 Itsukushima
3 Dazaifu
4 Naniwa (Ōsaka)
5 Heijō (Nara)
6 Heian (Kyōto)
7 Kamakura
8 Edo (Tōkyō)

1. The heavenly incidents relating the creation of world.
2. The north-western mythology, 'Izumo'.
3. The Imperial descent to earth.
4. The south-western mythology, 'Tsukushi' or 'Hiuga'.

The majority of the third type are continental in origin, and are associated with the second and with a subpart of the first. They were brought to Japan by the Imperial family groups, to whose tradition they of course belong. The remainder are of southern origin and are related primarily to rice cultivation in the Yayoi Period. They are earlier than the continental myths, so to accord with the linguistic chronology of the immigrations we must assume much earlier southern migrations, whether the settlers were cultivators or not. The mythologies are accounts of the affairs of the gods, anthropomorphized or personified, and yet it is possible to discern everywhere in the mythology and in the ancient poetry the unique belief in the anima, 'tama', as well as of the mana, 'chi', both belonging to earlier stages of the development of primitive mentality than the concept of a god, 'kami', and probably earlier than rice cultivation.

Sociological Foundations

Therefore the assumption of the presence in Neolithic Japan of inhabitants of Polynesian linguistic stocks may be correct. It seems difficult, however, to reconcile the apparent contradictions between the linguistic and mythological evidence, and that offered by physiological data on the contemporary Japanese, unless we allow ourselves one assumption: that the immigrants of southern stock were few in numbers, but that their migration washed over Japan recurrently, over a period of time; and that these migrants were of such cultural, and hence, economic, advancement as to be a continuing and powerful influence on Japanese culture and daily life.

Many of these assumptions seem to be gaining gradual acceptance in Japan, because in the north-western myths a cultural phase similar to that of the proto-cultivational southeast Asian one has been pointed out recently, and some archaeologists ac-knowledge the existence of a non-rice culture in Neolithic Japan. Moreover, some ethnologists have classified the traditional folklore of Japan into five cultural complexes, through comparative study: a matrilineal, fraternal society of taro cultivators and hunters; one of matrilineal hunters and upland rice cultivators; a male-dominated, ago-regimented society of rice growers and fishers; a patrilineal clan—the 'hara–of cultivators and hunters; and a monarchi-patriarchal kinship group, the 'uji'. The first three came to Japan spasmodically in the late Neolithic Period from the south, and the last two later, from the continent via Korea.

Continental immigrations took place constantly, from China as well as Korea, until the early historical period. All of the immigrants, including the older ones, have since been naturalized and absorbed into one hybrid Japanese race. As can be seen in maps of the very complicated distribution of bloodtypes and fingerprints, the contemporary hybrid has every conceivable variation of admixture, like the mosaic formation of the topography and the climate.

Plates

Burial Mound of Yamato-totohi-momoso-hime
(Nara Prefecture)

17 Momoso-hime was the wife of the god of Ōmiwa, and the aunt of the Emperor Sujin. Legend says that when the mound, called the Hashi-haka, was being built, many deities helped in the work under cover of night. 902′ long; 7.4 acres.

Burial Mound of the Emperor Sujin
(Nara Prefecture)

18 Sujin is recorded as the tenth Emperor of Japan in the 'Nihon-Shoki', an official history prepared in the Nara Period. He is now generally considered the founder of the first Yamato government, in the eastern part of the Yamato basin. The mound was built by cutting off the end of one arm of a folded mountain range, and was shaped with soil excavated from the surrounding moat. The mound is 786′ in length, and comprises 19.7 acres.

Burial Mound of Gobyōyama (Ōsaka Prefecture)

19 In the background the Burial Mound of the Emperor Richu; in the middle, that of Itasuke.

Ise Shrine, Naigū (Mie Prefecture)

20 Aerial view. To the right of the present shrine is one of the alternative sites for the shrine building. The building has been reconstructed, except for a few occasions, every twenty years since 690 A.D. At the center of this site there is a small hut housing the former buried sacred post, on which the next main shrine will be built with a new sacred post.

21 Isuzu River. The sacred river and Mt. Kamiji, the holy mountain. On this peak the sun goddess descended from heaven.

22 The sacred enclosure. The two buildings at the back of the main shrine are storehouses for sacred objects.

23 The Central Main Shrine. The two wooden-board roofs attached to the main shrine form a covered open space for ritual use.

Izumo Shrine (Shimane Prefecture)

24 The main shrine, corner view. The curve of the gable and roof contrasts with the straight lines of the roof of Ise Shrine. The roof at Izumo was probably influenced by Buddhist architecture, as were the other shrines.

25 The mighty posts of the surrounding veranda well express the monumental nature of this huge shrine building.

26 Main Shrine, rear view. The main shrine building is 79′ in height. The diagonal members, the 'chigi', are here merely decorative, while those at Ise are extensions of the actual gable rafters.

27 A corner of the veranda.

28 The entrance. The huge straw rope with tassels hanging over the entry forms the symbolic enclosure of the sacred place.

Itsukushima Shrine (Hiroshima Prefecture)

29 None but the priests and priestesses serving the shrine's deities were permitted to dwell on this sacred island in ancient times. The site was planned to place the axis of the compound along the axis of the bay. The yard behind the shrine, the Main Shrine, the Worship Hall, the Hall of Ritual Dances, the open platform for dance offerings, the 'torii'—the symbolic gate—in the sea, and the ritual site on the opposite shore, were all arranged on an axis aligned with the sacred mountain. The incorporation of the sea into the compound derived from the doctrines of the Jōdo sect of Buddhism, in which the Pure Land of Buddha—the Jōdo—is separated from this world by fire and water.

30 The winding walkways.

31 The colourful covered open spaces of the projecting Hall of Ritual Dances articulate the various spaces, while connecting the sections of the shrine. They form an organic composition in the manner of a fugue, with variation after variation on the basic theme.

32 View from the Hall of Ritual Dances to the opposite shore.

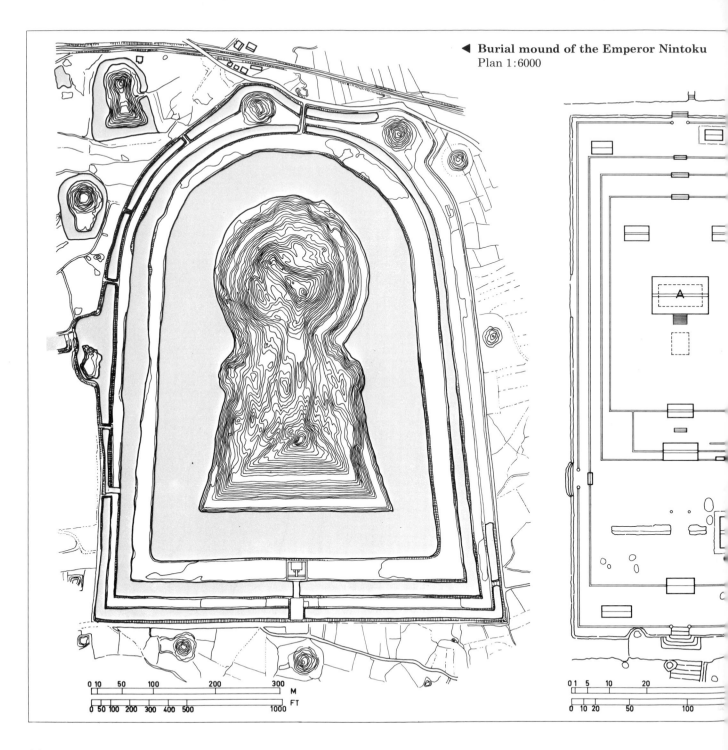

◄ Burial mound of the Emperor Nintoku
Plan 1:6000

0 10 50 100 200 300 M
0 50 100 200 300 400 500 1000 FT

0 1 5 10 20
0 10 20 50 100

14

Ise Temple
Plan-type 1:1000, plan, infrastructure and elevations 1:200

A shoden

Notes

Ō-miwa Shrine

The Nihon Shoki, the Chronicle of Japan, relates that the Emperor Sujin, who is usually credited with founding the Yamato government, worshipped the sun goddes, Amaterasu, in the sacred 'shiki' enclosure, and the Yamato earth spirit on the shrine's sacred hill. He then made obeisances to O-mono-nushi, also known as Ō-miwa, the master of all spirits, who dwelt in Mount Miwa. The marriage of the spirit O-mono-nushi to the female ancestor of the Miwa clan is also recorded in the Chronicle, and many clans trace their ancestry to the marriages of deities which appear in the classics.

A similar sacred nuptial takes place in the traditions of the Kamo Shrine, in Kyōto, which has been transformed into an ancient ritual which is practiced even today. One daughter of the Kamo clan is dedicated as a priestess to the guardian god. She attends at midnight on an April night, beside an enclosure containing a sacred bough, and prays to the deity to descend to the bough through the sacred hill. This ceremony is probably a ritualization of ancient Japanese fertility rites, other evidences of which are found in many of the relics excavated from the tumuli, and other sources.

Itsukushima Shrine

Mandō-e: The Buddhist Ritual of 10,000 Lanterns. In the Fall of 1177, Prime Minister Taira Kiyomori presided over a nocturnal Buddhist festival of lanterns at Itsukushima Shrine. Nearly 1000 Buddhist priests, and many aristocrats and ladies of the court, participated. The Hall of Worship and the Hall of Sacred Dances were filled with richly attired aristocrats, while the priests, clad in lavish robes of damask, gold, and silver, occupied the 120 bays of the labyrinthine covered passageways. Lamps were lit, and the celebrants hung countless lanterns from the eaves of the shrine; a line of bonfires was arranged parallelling the rear passage. Piles were driven into the floor of the sea across the mouth of Itsukushima Bay, on a line with the great red 'torii', and a fire was placed atop each. A line of fires was arrayed along over a quarter-mile of the opposite shore of the strait, and many fire-bearing boats floated in the strait and the bay, so that the water itself seemed to burn with the reflection.

Chants of Buddhist scriptures echoed from the steep mountain-side and the waters of the bay, bringing to the participants a vision of the Buddha's Pure Land Paradise.

Ise Shrine

The study of Ise Shrine is, in fact, the study of prehistoric Japanese religions, because Ise represents, quite simply, the accumulation of them all, from the most primitive to the most developed. It has been possible to reconstruct the original rites, through analysis of the rituals performed there now. The primordial rite consisted of a priestess, worshipping beside a sacred planted bough, which received the guardian deity when she descended from heaven. Sanctified at Ise are a hill, a bush, water and stones, a sacred mirror, the sacred pillar, which is half-buried beneath the floor of the shrine. Along with the Imperial Ancestor Deity, deities of the sun, the wind, and fertility are believed to reside here.

Ise is unique in that it incorporates two separate main shrines: The Naigū, or inner shrine, is for the sanctification of Amaterasu, who is the Imperial Ancestor and sun goddess. The Gegū, or outer shrine, is the shrine of Toyuke-hime, the goddess of fertility and food, who was the deity of the indigenous Ise clan. Historians cite the exterior, or subordinate, position of the fertility shrine as evidence that the Ise clan were subjugated by the Yamato clan, whose deity was then assigned an accordingly superior position.

Sacred Mirrors

Bronze mirrors, which had been imported from China in Neolithic times, were traditionally sacred objects, and were interred with the dead in ancient funerary rites. They were also employed in the subjugation rituals recorded in the Japanese classics. The sacred bronze bells–'sanagi', or 'dōtaku'–which were buried in the mountains in ancient rites, have no Continental antecedents, however, and are of prehistoric Japanese origin. These bells have appeared in many archaeological excavations, and there is ample evidence that they were used in rituals at Suwa and Ise shrines, and elsewhere. There are no references to 'dōtaku' in the mythology or folklore, however, so that the bells may be taken as evidence of a culture and rituals antedating the ancient Yamato Imperial tradition.

27

31

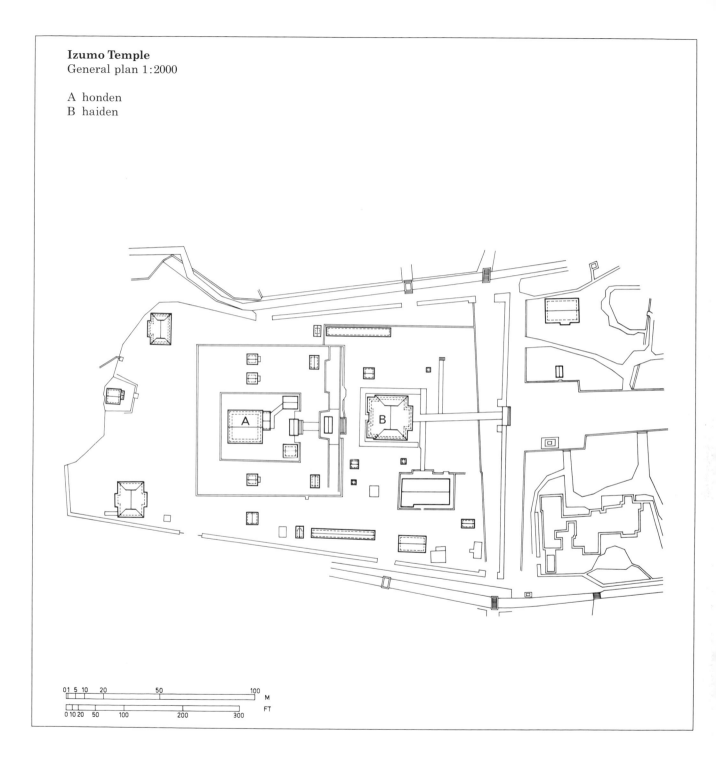

Izumo Temple
General plan 1:2000

A honden
B haiden

01 5 10   20   50   100
                                          M
0 10 20 50   100   200   300
                                     FT

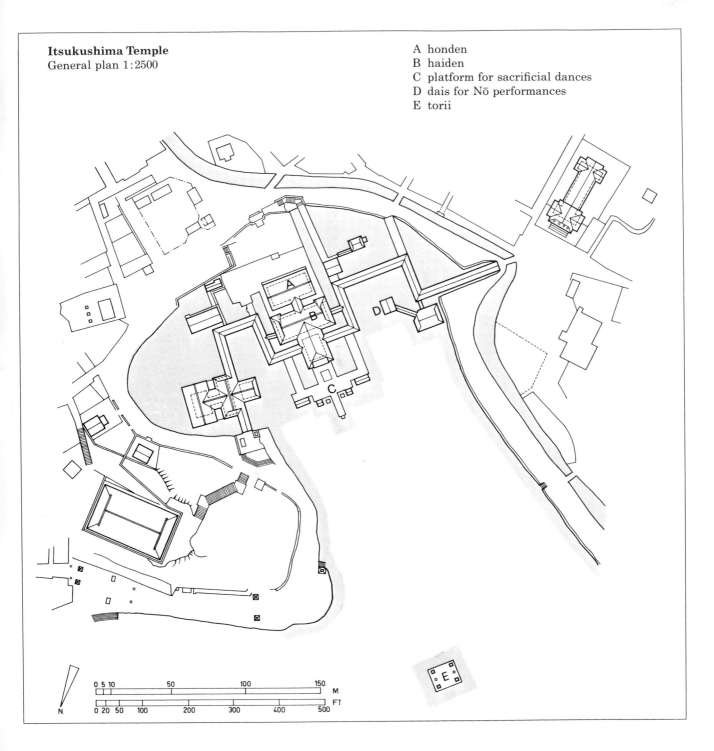

Itsukushima Temple
General plan 1:2500

A honden
B haiden
C platform for sacrificial dances
D dais for Nō performances
E torii

0 5 10   50   100   150 M
0 20 50 100   200   300   400 500 FT

N.

1. General History

Jōmon Period

The Neolithic period of Japan is called the Jōmon Earthernware Period, and is chronologically divided into five sub-periods according to the various styles of earthenware excavated from over 2,000 shell mounds. The term 'Jōmon' means 'rope-mark', and refers to the decoration characteristic of the earthenware of the period, in which cords were pressed into the surface of the clay before firing, leaving an impression in the fired ware. Carbon 14 tests of shells in the lowest layers of the mounds indicate that the earliest period was c. 10,000 to 600 B.C.

Around 10,000 B.C. the Japanese Islands were shifting from a diluvial to an alluvial epoch, and the lower plains which are now under rice cultivation were still marshes, or under sea level. The inhabitants were nomadic families or small groups settled near the sea or the rivers who lived by fishing, hunting small animals, and gathering fresh-water and sea shells and fruit. Bones of whales and other ocean fish excavated from the settlements of this period indicate the existence of boats and organized ocean fishing, but there is no evidence of husbandry. The most densely populated area was the end of the diluvial plateau in the eastern part of the central mountain range of Japan, that is, the present Kantō district and Yamanashi Prefecture.

Yayoi Period

The culture of the Eneolithic or Yayoi Earthenware Period, from about the third century B.C., was fundamentally different from that of the preceding Neolithic Jōmon Period. Yayoi is the place name of the site in Tōkyō where this type of earthenware was discovered for the first time.

The Yayoi culture first developed in the north of Kyushu, that part of Japan nearest to the continent, and gradually spread eastward to the Kawachi Plain, Nara Basin, Yamashiro Basin, and other areas in the Kinki district where the half dry, low-lying land was suitable for rice cultivation, and where the first imperial authority was later established. This eastern movement was due in part to the presence of wide fertile plains and basins to the east of Ōsaka Bay, and partly to fear of attack from the Korean peninsula. Agricultural implements were made of iron, while ritual utensils such as mirrors, bells – called 'dōtaku' – spearheads and sabres were made of bronze. Chinese records of this time state that the higher classes in Japan were polygamous and lived in pit dwellings; only the most exalted persons built two storied houses. A settlement of about 130 pit dwellings has been excavated in Karako, Nara Prefecture, and about 200 round-cornered pit dwellings have been excavated in Kugawara, Tōkyō. In Toro, in Shizuoka Prefecture, a grid of rice fields, ½ to ¾ acre each in area, has been discovered, along with a group of twelve pit dwellings, and two storehouses elevated on stilts.

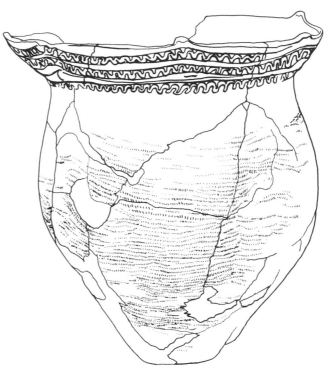

Pottery, Yayoi period

Pottery, Jōmon period

Kofun Period

Many burial mounds were constructed from about the third century A.D. until the introduction of Buddhism in the sixth century, when cremation became the universal funerary practice. These mounds, later known as 'kofun', gave their name to that period.

The earliest unit of social organization was a clan, the union of several families or a family complex called 'uji', having one common family and place name. The general name of such a settlement was 'mura', which originally meant 'group', and the larger organization of the surrounding land and the people was called 'kuni'. Each 'uji' had a guardian god, or 'uji-gami', which was worshipped by the adult members of the group. The 'uji' was ruled politically and religiously by a chief called 'uji-no-kami', whose death was a serious crisis for the 'uji', and was marked by a grand funeral rite and the construction of a huge burial mound by the collective labour of the group.

The 'kofun' were at first merely ritual burial places of the leader of an 'uji', but as several 'uji' united to collaborate on irrigating the wide plains for rice cultivation, the 'kofun' came to be a powerful political and religious symbol of the emerging nation. Grad-

ually one group of 'uji' gained political and military supremacy, and established the first imperial government at Yamato in the present Nara Prefecture. Their burial 'kofun' symbolized the absolute authority of the emperor.

Around the fifth century there was a hereditary system of rank called 'uji-kabane' in the area under imperial control, that is, Yamato, Kawachi and Yamashiro, or the present Kinki District. This system had

Ise Temple: general plan
1 Shōden   2 Naigu

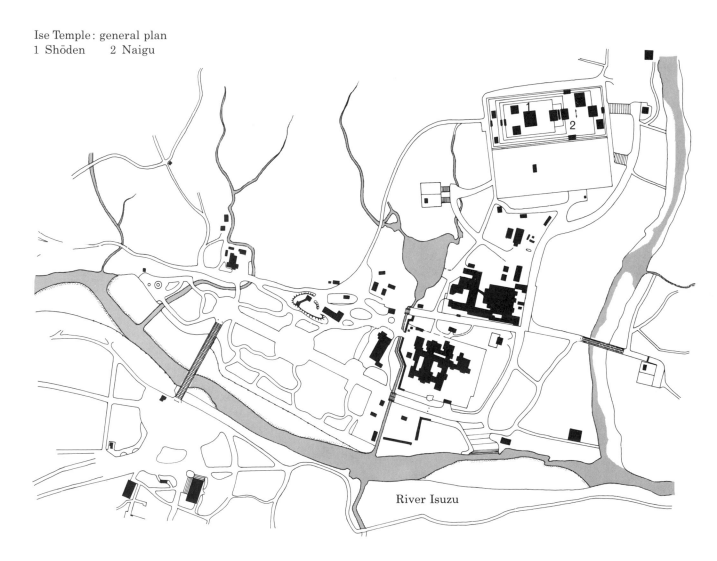

River Isuzu

probably been imported from the kingdom of Silla, in Korea, between the third and fourth centuries, during the transitional period from the Yayoi to the Kofun era.

The 'agata-nushi', the governor of the lands belonging to the Imperial household, and 'tomo-no-miyakko', the leader of the group of workers called 'tomo-be', belonging to the Imperial family, were appointed from among the influential clans.

In the fifth century, the golden age of the Kofun Period, the government was in the hands of two administrators, the 'Ō-omi', the leader of the Omi group of landlords in the south-west of the Yamato basin and the 'Ō-muraji', the leader of the Muraji group of 'tomo-no-miyakko'. These were the two highest ranks in the 'kabane' system next to the 'O-kimi', or Emperor, chief of the 'kimi', or Imperial family. Later the families which held the title of 'omi' were considered descendants of the Imperial line. Those who held the title of 'muraji' as descendants of different ancestral gods, were considered relatives of the Imperial ancestor god.

After the middle of the fifth century, clans outside the sphere of influence of the Imperial authority grew in strength. Hence a new system of hereditary provincial governors, called 'kuni-no-miyakko' replaced the 'agata-nushi' system.

They were originally appointed from the influential clans, including the 'agata-nushi', and controlled the provinces both religiously and politically, performing religious rites and collecting taxes and corvées from the people under their control. They became more powerful than the old 'agata-nushi', some of whom still retained merely their titles. However, in A.D. 701, the Taiho Edict transferred the political control of the provinces to government officers called 'kuni-no-tsukasa', who functioned as part of a central bureaucracy. The old 'kuni-no-miyakko' were reduced to the status of priests of their traditional provincial and family guardian gods. Among these family guardian gods there were the great gods of Ise, Sumiyoshi, Yamato, and Izumo, which were all compelled to submit to the authority of the Yamato government. The great god of Ise was called Amaterasu-o-mikami, the glorious heaven goddess, and became the national guardian god. Ise was identified with the ancestral god of the Imperial family, which at the time maintained a strong government over the nation through the bureaucratic system in Yamato. Thus the old rituals of worship of the archaic local guardian god of Ise were buried under the new ceremonies of the national cult of Amaterasu.

The Introduction of Buddhism

Between the fifth century, the Yayoi Period, and the eighth century, by which time the political centre of the country was already in Nara, there were five waves of immigration across the sea route, and many workers and artisans from China and Korea settled in Japan. One of the most significant groups of immigrants in the making of Japan were those who brought new skills, that is, the pottery makers, weavers, iron workers, etc. These 'imaki-no-tebito' contributed to political and military organization, to the manufacture of artifacts and the expansion of trade.

However, their most important cultural contribution was the introduction of the Chinese system of writing. There is evidence that Chinese characters were in use as early as the fifth century. Two professional groups of calligraphers and linguists lived in Yamato and Kawachi: the 'ayahito', or foreigners, and the 'fubito', the writers.

At first the Chinese characters were used phonetically in writing the Japanese language, but sometimes they were used ideographically, to express their own original meaning – but read with the Japanese pronunciation. This has led to an ambiguity in early written Japanese, and has made it difficult to understand ancient records since the characters must be read sometimes phonetically and sometimes as ideograms. This has also influenced Japanese thought, strengthening the Japanese ability to express literarily subtle shades of feeling and abstract thought. With the infusion of Chinese linguistic influences into Japanese, there was a marked increase in the incidence of synonyms, while the adaptation of Chinese words to the essentially Polynesian phonetic structure of Japanese gave rise to a great many homophones. The addition of an entirely new vocabulary vastly increased the complexity and subtlety of the language. Chinese became the language for all official documents, and even as late as the eighteenth century was widely used as the language of scholarship. The pure native words of the Yamato culture, however, continued to survive in songs, poetry, 'Shintō' prayers, and other forms, and are still extant.

The immigrants' other major contribution to Japanese life was the introduction of Buddhism. For political reasons, a king of Paekche, in Korea, sent the Japanese Emperor Kimmei an image of the Buddha and a scroll of 'sutras'—scriptures—in A.D. 538. A long and serious quarrel between the 'Ō-omi' of the Soga clan and the 'Ō-muraji' of the Mononobe clan, the two families who traditionally administered the nation, developed over acceptance of the new religion, as they competed for political hegemony. Buddhism's first adherents in Japan were the immigrants who had settled in the Takechi district, in the southern Yamato Basin, which was also the home country of the Soga clan.

Buddhism gained general acceptance through the support of the 'Ō-omi', the leaders of this clan, although their followers were offered no promise of spiritual enlightenment. They regarded Buddhism not as a religion, or even a philosophy, but rather as a magic-religious cult in the tradition of the native Japanese guardian gods. However the arts of this Asuka Period were Buddhist, secularized and exotic, emotionally alien to the Japanese. Later, Buddhism was strongly supported by the Prince-Regent, Shōtoku Taishi (574–622), who studied Buddhist doctrine and the Chinese classics, and hoped to realize the Pure Land of Buddhism through constitutional law.

By the end of the Nara Period, at the end of the eighth century, six sects of Buddhism had established themselves in Nara. Judging from their basic doctrines, they had been established in the Sui Dynasty and early T'ang Dynasty in China. The ancient Japanese priests studied the doctrines in Chinese, with commentaries by Chinese priests, but their study was speculative in character, and they did not dispense the teachings or benefits of the new religion to the people. Only later, in the early Heian Period, were the Tendai and Shingon sects, with their promises of secular benefits, imported and practiced among the common people.

In 685, an Imperial Edict promulgated by the Emperor Temmu requested the people to construct Buddhist altars in their houses, and to worship and make offerings to them. In 741, a second edict, by the Emperor Shōmu, ordered the construction of provincial temples throughout Japan, and he began to erect the monumental Tōdai-ji temple in Nara as the central temple of the nation. With the promulgation of this edict, Buddhism may be said to have gained acceptance as the national religion. It grew in political importance until at last the capital had to be removed from Nara to Nagaoka by the aristocrats, to escape the power of the great temples.

Ritsuryō Period

In 646, the Taika Reform was proclaimed and executed. Private ownership of land and people by the aristocrats and local magnates was abolished, and all land reverted to the State. The construction of a new capital for the central government was proposed, a new provincial government organization was drawn up, and such communication facilities as stations, barriers, and guardposts were planned. A census was taken and the land allotments recorded in the registry. The old customs of tribute and corvée were replaced by a new taxation system. This edict firmly established the authority of the Yamato government, which had been founded in the middle of the Yayoi Period and had grown in strength through the disputes of the Kofun Period. The Imperial government proclaimed new laws—the Taihō Code in 702 and the Yōrō Code in 757—and for two centuries Japan was ruled directly by the Imperial autocracy, until land ownership gradually reverted to private hands. This is known as the Ritsuryō—or constitutional law—Period; 'ritsu' means criminal law and 'ryō' means civil law. The period corresponds to the Asuka, Nara and early Heian periods of art history, all of which were named after their capital cities.

These codes were established with the help of scholars who were sent to Sui and T'ang China by the Yamato government to study Chinese institutions, since the traditional customary laws of the clans were inadequate to govern the united clans, and a new bureaucratic system had to be set up.

The Japanese codes generally followed the Chinese system except that the government was not organized in a complete pyramid as in China, but was divided at the top between the 'Jingi-kan', the minister in charge of traditional gods, and the 'Dajō-kan', the prime minister of secular politics. The 'Jingi-kan' probably enjoyed more power than the 'Dajō-kan' because of the traditional importance of ceremonies for the gods.

Another important difference concerned the laws relating to cultivated fields, 'ta', which in China referred to every kind of cultivation, but in Japan only referred to the rice fields. Chinese law allowed heirs to retain two-lengths of a man's alloted land after his death, but Japanese law required that it all be returned to the government. Thus the Yamato government sought to establish strict control by adapting the Chinese laws and bureaucratic system to conditions in Japan. The allotment of fields under the Taika Reform took place in 652.

After 721, people who reclaimed wasteland were rewarded with official ranks. This was encouraged to overcome the shortage of arable fields available for allotment, a shortage due largely to special grants of land made to officials according to their rank, and to those who performed distinguished service. However, this practice was restricted in 729. Before this, in 723, a new edict had allowed the family of a man who reclaimed land to possess it for three generations. This idea was contrary to the original idea of public land and probably resulted both from unfamiliarity with constitutional law, and from the Japanese tendency to change their attitudes towards the law as the situation dictates.

In 743, five years after maps of the provinces and districts were ordered to be drawn up, an edict was proclaimed which allowed the permanent possession of any lands reclaimed within three years. This eventually caused the collapse of the whole Ritsuryō System. The amount of private land permitted was limited according to the official rank of the owners; thus aristocrats, shrines, temples and local magnates collected large areas of fields and ruled over them. The Government could not collect any revenue from such land, and the peasants on government fields gradually left and went to work on private land to escape the heavier burden of taxation.

Under the Taihō Code of 702, the land was divided for administrative purposes into 'kuni', provinces, then 'kōri', districts, and the smallest units, sato, villages, which were originally natural settlements, but were legally defined as units of thirty households. This last classification was reorganized, in 715, into legal units of fifty households called 'go-ko', which were subdivided into 'ri', settlements, to correspond with the actual villages. The 'go-ko' was the unit responsible for taxation and was composed of a number of 'bō-ko' or families. However, these formal regulations hardly coincided with the actual situation since, as the population of one 'go-ko' increased, the number of fields alloted to it had to be increased. Thus the number of government fields were continually decreasing as more and more land passed into the hands of private owners, making the reallotment of land every six years, as required by the Taika Reform, more and more difficult. The reclamation policies originally initiated to solve this problem only served to aggravate it.

Private landlords' holdings grew ever larger, and the practice arose of dedicating the land to an influential shrine, temple or aristocrat, even to the Imperial family – institutions exempt from taxation – while the landlords became supervisors, ensuring their continued private profit. Eventually even the original government fields, which had fallen into disuse, were reclaimed and collected by the landlords. The most influential family, the Fujiwara, who were the descendants of the original author of the Taika Reform, emerged as the most politically powerful and ruled as dictators despite the Ritsuryō institution. Disputes often occurred, even within a single influential family, over the succession and ownership of land, and these disputes, coupled with the disintegration of the government militia, were instrumental in the emergence of the warrior class.

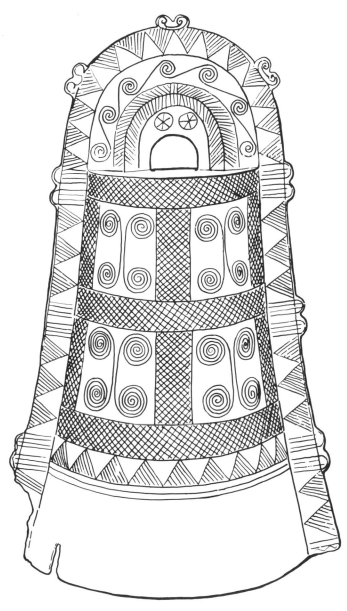

'Dōtaku', bronze bell of the Yayoi period

Shōen: the Manor

The great number of privately owned fields in the eighth century were called 'shō' or 'shōen'. Origin-ally, 'shō' meant a compound of houses, storehouses and vegetable plots, but later this was called 'shōke' and the compound and the cultivated fields around it were called 'shōen'. These were owned by important temples or shrines, or such aristocrats as the Fuji-wara family, but were supervised by wardens, who were appointed by the owners. Later these wardens were replaced by local magnates, who actually owned much of the land, but dedicated it to the temples and shrines in order to avoid taxation. The magnates had no formal status under the Ritsuryō provincial gov-ernment.

In 794, the capital was removed from Nara to Heian-Kyō, the present-day Kyōto. The early half of the Heian Period was called the Sekkan Period, after the administrative system of the central government, a very different one from the older Ritsuryō bureau-cracy. The Fujiwara family controlled national affairs as 'sesshō', or regent, when the emperor was a child, and as 'kanpaku', advisor, when he became a youth. From the latter half of the ninth century, the Fujiwara family maintained consanguinity with the Imperial family through the marriage of their daughters to the emperor. The succession of emperors was arrang-ed by the Fujiwara grandfather, continuing political dominance by the Fujiwaras until the eleventh cen-tury. The family monopolized all the important posi-tions at court and in government.

The 'Daigoku-den', the great hall of national admi-nistration, burned down accidentally several times after the ninth century. Affairs of state were con-sequently removed to the 'Shishin-den', the main hall of the emperor's private living quarters, and gov-erning the nation became the private affair of the emperor. The 'Shishin-den' itself also caught fire twenty-six times in the tenth and eleventh centuries, and the emperor had to move to the residence of his grandfather – a Fujiwara – on each occasion, because there was no 'Daigoku-den'. Thus the private admi-nistration of the nation by the emperor became the private administration by the Fujiwara family. The emperor was merely a figurehead, performing nation-al and religious rites as a priest for the traditional gods.

To be appointed regent or advisor, however, was

not easy, since the 'sesshō' or 'kanpaku' had to be 'uji-no-chōja', the chief of the family who ruled over the Fujiwara 'shōen'; his wife had to bear a daughter as the future wife of the emperor, and this daughter, after marriage to the emperor, had to bear a son as a future emperor. If any one of these conditions was not fulfilled the title passed to another branch of the Fujiwara family. The changes wrought by this situation in the family led to the continual fragmentation of its vast privileges and property.

In the latter half of the eleventh century, after two-hundred years of Sekkan government, a crisis shattered the Fujiwara suzerainty. In 1186, the Emperor Shirakawa abdicated in favor of his seven-year-old son, Horikawa, while taking the tonsure, and continuing to rule from 'retirement'.

Thus abdicated emperors, as the heads of the Imperial family, with vast property, held political power greater than the emperor's; this system of imperial government was called 'insei', and the period, the Insei Period. In the Sekkan Period the emperors had acted as the symbolic figurehead of government, but in the Insei Period even this function was assumed by the abdicated emperor, not by the emperor himself. The Imperial family had also become merely another aristocratic family whose authority was threatened by the warriors of powerful 'shōen', since the old constitutional law was completely ignored.

Around the eleventh century tenants – called 'tato' – undertook the cultivation of the 'shōen' for the real landowners, paying rents in kind and service for the privilege. Later this tax was imposed not on the men but on the fields and called 'tato-yaku', binding people to the land. Toward the end of the eleventh century these fields came to be known as 'myōden', and the landlords as 'myōshu'.

In this 'myō' system, which had fully developed by the middle of the twelfth century in the older central districts, the rice fields, vegetable plots, and building compounds were included as former 'shōen'. The scale of the 'myōden' in those districts of relatively dense settlement was never large enough to allow the 'tato' or 'myōshu' to become very powerful. But in the outer districts there were a lot of 'daimyōshu', or great landlords, who controlled large areas, and

who were eventually appointed as local government officers because of their economic power. They further appropriated the few remaining government fields.

In the event of conflicts between the local land-lords – the 'myōshu' or 'daimyō' – and the real land-owners (who might even be the Imperial family), the former had to protect their interests by force. Warrior bands grew up around these local landlords, which at first resembled the earlier 'uji' type of family. Some of these bands later united, forming local groups called 'ikki', which literally means riot, and these in turn finally were organized into a system of vassals and lords, from which the first military government, in Kamakura, was formed in 1192. Then warriors were appointed to the local governorships called 'jitō', who were officially government officers, but they swore loyalty not to the legal government in Heian-kyo but to the 'Shōgun', Minamoto Yoritomo, that is, the 'Kamakura-no-dono' or leader of the military government. The warriors were his 'go-kenin', household retainers, and in return for their loyalty they were granted by the 'Shōgun' the privilege of holding their native lands, 'honryō', as 'myō-shu', and collecting regular profits for themselves.

The Kamakura military government also instituted a provincial police system in which one of the influential 'jitō' in each district was appointed as the chief, 'shugo', or protector. He derived no income from this post; his job was to prevent revolts or murders, and to ensure that the 'jitō' carried out the Shogun's will.

There were many 'myōshu' who did not become 'go-kenin', or direct vassals of the Kamakura 'Shōgun', but still retained their traditional control of the 'shōen'. They were vassals, rather, of the old owner, or his appointee, and had no feudatory link to the Kamakura government. In those districts where the Kamakura government had appointed 'jitō', disputes often arose between him and the 'myōshu' for control of the 'myōden'; in most cases, the 'jitō' won, since these disputes were adjudicated by the 'shugo', who also owed loyalty – and position – to Kamakura. When the 'shugo' himself became involved in such a dispute, there was no one to resolve it, but the effect of this system was to increasingly concentrate power in the hands of the 'jitō', 'shugo', and the Kamakura government, ultimately reducing all others to the status of hired cultivators, and laying the foundations for later feudal society.

Court Culture

Following three centuries of vigorous court life, the Imperial family had become debilitated, the court culture decadent by the Sekkan Period. The aristocrats were filled with fears and forebodings, since Buddhism taught that the world without salvation had come. For the first time Buddhism touched the human soul in Japan, though even then in an aesthetic rather than a religious way, and the rituals of a mystic school of Tantric Buddhism were performed at court. The construction of temples in the suburbs of the capital became fashionable among the Imperial family and the court aristocracy.

The 'Shingon-shū', one sect of this school, taught that all phenomena in nature reveal the omnipresence of Maha-Vairocana, the highest Buddha; every visible object is the body of this Buddha, every sound his voice, and the whole of existence is but a manifestation of his thought. A man could only perceive this reality by identifying himself with the body, words, and thought of the Buddha through ascetic practices, performing secret rituals before a painted scroll of Buddhist images.

However, the court nobles performed those rituals – called 'kitō' – only for personal profit, although the mystic atmosphere in the temples, some of which were beautifully finished and dedicated by the aristocrats, seemed to manifest the actual presence of Buddha.

Another school which gained popularity was the Jōdo Sect, which preached that after death believers would enter the Pure Land of Amitabha, the Buddha of Boundless Light. The promise of eternal salvation appealed to the court nobles who were being deprived of worldly power by the growing authority of the warriors in the provinces.

The resultant atmosphere of court culture and religions – introverted, melancholic, and uncertain – was reflected in the literature of the court ladies who wrote about their innermost feelings. The aesthetic of the period, 'mono-no-aware', developed a mood of delicate humour and melancholic pathos, perhaps best exemplified in Lady Murasaki Shikibu's eleventh century romance, 'The Tale of Genji'. In her novel, Murasaki deals adeptly with the delicate moods of the ladies of the Court, with their intrigues, and with the effeteness of the Court itself. 'Genji', like many other works of the period, was written largely in 'kana', a cursive writing style in which the brush rarely leaves the paper; it was considered 'women's writing' especially as it was thought to reflect women's constantly changing moods.

The Rise of the Warrior Bands: the Turbulent Age

In ancient times the chief of a family was called the 'uji-no-kami', and in the Sekkan Period, the 'uji-no-chōja'. The 'Sesshō' or 'Kanpaku' had to be the 'uji-no-chōja' of the Fujiwara family; the emperor was the 'uji-no-chōja' of the Imperial family, and inherited vast 'shōen'. He controlled the Imperial family, with the exception of those branch families whose leaders occupied such important government positions as the 'Dajō-daijin' – the prime minister – the two ministers of the Right and Left, or governors of the provinces. The same situation prevailed in the Fujiwara family, and these two families competed between themselves for influence during the Heian Period. Within each family, the position of 'uji-no-chōja' was sought by all the branches, and from the middle of the ninth century many disputes arose over clan leadership.

The desire for private land, the 'shōen', and the appropriation of private lands by the local magnates and warriors caused unrest throughout Japan. Members of the two leading families, the Fujiwara and the Imperial family, who had been sent to the provinces as governors, became bandits or pirates rather than return to the capital and live in humbler circumstances after their appointments expired. During the tenth century these bands infested the seas and the countryside.

Even during the Kofun Period, when the Yamato

Political map of ancient Japan

1 Izumo
2 Yamashiro
3 Kawachi
4 Ise
5 Yamato

Hokkaidō

Kantō

1

Chūgoku

Kinki

2

3 4

5

Shikoku

Kyūshū

government was first established, riots had occurred in the Kibi District, present-day Okayama, and in Kyūshū. During the Ritsuryō Period, the government sent troops under a 'Sei-i-dai-shōgun' – a commanding general – to establish military headquarters in the north-east, and to quell the frequent uprisings there. Later, during the tenth century, other headquarters were established in the eastern regions and elsewhere to quell the disturbances, but these were under the command of generals appointed from famous families, the most important of whom were the Heike, the leading family of the Taira clan, and the Genji, the leader of Minamoto, both of imperial lineage. In the latter half of the twelfth century disputes over the 'shōen', and over the inheritances of the great families of the capital, Heian-kyō', became more frequent. In 1167, Taira Kiyomori was appointed 'Dajō-Daijin' and the Taira family quickly eclipsed the Fujiwara, who had dominated the court and the government for two centuries.

In 1185, the Taira were defeated by Minamoto Yoritomo, who united the eastern warrior bands under his leadership, and established a military government at Kamakura, far from the turbulent Imperial capital. This was, in fact, a victory of the local wardens, usurping the power of the absentee landlords, members of the central aristocracy of the decadent 'myōshu' system. However, this was not the end of disputes over land, which continued through the Middle Ages, until an absolute feudal system was established by the Tokugawa clan at the beginning of the seventeenth century. Bandits continued to infest the country, and serious disputes between the Imperial family and the Kamakura government, in 1221, led to the abdication of one emperor, and the exile of three ex-emperors, upon the orders of the military government.

In the latter half of the thirteenth century Mongolian troops invaded Kyūshū; for the first time since the establishment of a government in Japan, external forces threatened. All factions, warriors, aristocrats, shrines and temples, united to repel the attack. This new sense of solidarity among different groups may have helped cause a new type of riot in which peasants united with the local landlords to plunder the

a) 'Dogū', Jomon period
b) 'Dogū', Yayoi period

few remaining fields which still belonged to the central authorities.

The so-called 'Nanboku Chō', in the fourteenth century, the period of Northern and Southern Imperial Courts, was a result of the power struggle between the warriors and the aristocrats, who sought to regain their former authority. Both sides tried to gain the support of the bandits, and for a time, the aristocrats held the Kamakura government at bay, and the Imperial government recovered its authority. However, Ashikaga Takauji, who had revolted against the Kamakura government and helped the aristocrats, turned against the emperor and succeeded in forming a warrior's government in the Muromachi section of Kyōto.

In the countryside, the native lower classes had gained new power and new figures gradually assumed positions of authority of their own accord, privately owning and ruling the land and people in several provinces. This was the simplest and most direct form of land ownership. The authority of the Muromachi government was gradually dissolved and the traditional influence of the Imperial family and the Ashikaga clan all but disappeared, retaining only a symbolic function. The emperor still appointed men of power to the positions of minister, advisor, or commanding general of the ancient – but now illusory – Imperial government. The new ruler had to possess vast domains in order to support large military expeditions far from his base – expeditions now well supplied with firearms and other weapons – and support professional soldiers who had long since ceased to cultivate the fields themselves.

Oda Nobunaga had all these qualifications, but his rise to a position of suzerainty was terminated when a revolt by one of his vassals led to his death. He was succeeded by Toyotomi Hideyoshi, who was born the son of a peasant, but rose to high rank as a vassal of Oda Nobunaga. After Nobunaga's death, he eventually became the ruler of the country and was appointed 'Kanpaku' – advisor to the emperor – in 1585, and then 'Dajō-daijin' – prime minister – by the emperor, thus symbolically confirming his power. With the confiscation of arms from the peasants to prevent the formation of bands of robbers, he rigidly fixed the professions on a hereditary basis, dividing peasants, craftsmen and merchants. He ordered a survey of the country, called the 'Taikō-kenchi', in which a census was taken and every cultivated field was measured on a standardized scale; the potential yield of each field for the various crops was estimated according to the richness of the soil. From this time onward, peasants were bound to their fields more rigidly, as the class responsible for cultivation, and were the sole base on which taxes were levied. Feudal lords were appointed by Hideyoshi to collect the taxes. It was also their responsibility to produce the estimated crops from their provinces and to render any requested services, including military aid, to Hideyoshi. Thus feudalism was established in Japan; Hideyoshi was succeeded by Tokugawa Ieyasu, who was appointed the 'Seii-dai-shōgun', or commanding general, by the emperor, and founded a new capital and government in Edo, the present-day Tōkyō.

Medieval Culture

The Medieval Period was a time of transition from the rigid society under the Chinese laws imported in the seventh century, to a freer, more vital way of life. Although later society was strictly organized into classes, within the class system there was great freedom of expression, especially among the wealthy merchant class. This freedom developed during the turbulent ages of war when the old laws and customs were broken down. Some ancient traditions disappeared and others were absorbed and transformed by medieval ideas.

The new culture of the later Sung Dynasty, especially Zen (Ch'an) Buddhism, was imported and flourished during the Medieval Era. New patterns of life were being formed by the newly risen warrior class and the urban commoners, whose fresh and dynamic attitudes contrasted with the decadent delicacy of the declining aristocracy. The turbulent battles and fluid social situation caused the mixing and refining of the imported and traditional cultures which produced a culture of an extremely ascetic character.

The unrest made for great mobility, so that one such as Hideyoshi, the son of a peasant, might finally rise to unify the country under his own rule. It was his ability to collect together the bands of warriors as his vassals, then to provide the necessary equipment for battle, and finally to receive from the emperor the

'Haniwa' terra-cotta model of house (Yayoi period)

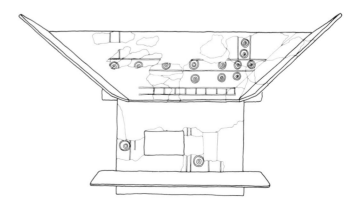

title of 'Shōgun', or an imperial command, which allowed him to wage war against his rivals.

False ancient genealogies were often assumed by the 'daimyō' and influential landlords who sought appointment to a position in the Imperial shadow government, since justice was considered to invest in the ancient authorities. The warriors and even wealthy merchants could participate in the traditional culture, which before had been the sole prerogative of members of the aristocratic class who now sold their techniques of Waka poems, calligraphy and other traditional culture for as high a price as possible to the aspiring warriors and merchants. These transactions led to a broad dispersal of cultural activities throughout the country and to every class of society. Many distinguished masters of medieval arts – painters, Nō-players, gardeners, tea masters, etc. – came from the lower classes of society. Even a low peasant could become an 'ashigaru' – infantryman – with a single spear, and if he distinguished himself in battle he could rise to a full warrior, and with ability and good fortune, a 'daimyō'. Before the end of the Medieval Period, when the class structure was formalized, many 'daimyō' rose to this high position from a low class family background.

The commoner classes could also enter the Buddhist priesthood, which before had been an exclusively aristocratic calling, and rise to the abbotcy of one of the many temples which had been constructed and dedicated by local magnates throughout Japan. The priests of the influential temples often wielded power equalling that of many lords, or gained their patronage, along with some of the more prominent and fashionable poets and artists of the day.

The Medieval Era had a strongly religious tone. Previous court culture had made religion aesthetic, but in medieval times even secular arts had a religious character, and the sense of beauty was influenced by religion, especially Buddhist philosophy.

Hōnen, the founder of the Jōdo Sect of Buddhism, was the son of a provincial sheriff. In 1198, at the age of sixty-six, he propounded the doctrine that those who wish for rebirth in paradise need only recite the name of Amitabha Buddha and have faith in the fulfilled promise of Amitabha that he would not himself become Buddha until all people were saved. His disciple, Shinran, carried his master's thought one step further, teaching that the mere recitation of Amitabha Buddha's name guaranteed salvation, since salvation did not depend on self but only on the promise of Amitabha. Thus the will to pray to Amitabha was identified with Amitabha's promise to save, a logic of transferring one's merit or virtue to others to attain Buddhahood – a concept called 'Ekō'.

The Amitabha and other 'Nenbutsu' sects, sects which invoked the name of a Buddha as a means of salvation, developed from the Jodo doctrine, which had been studied in Japan since ancient times, while the Zen Sect developed from doctrines introduced at the end of the ancient period and at the beginning of the Medieval Era.

Dōgen, founder of the Sōtō School of Zen in Japan, was the son of an aristocrat. He studied Buddhism in the Tendai Sect temples of Mt. Hiei, but began to question their doctrines, which taught that man is born as a Buddha. If this were so, he asked, why should man live an ascetic life in order to achieve spiritual enlightenment? His dissatisfaction led him to China, where he studied under the master Ju-ch'ing, and attained enlightenment: man is not born as a Buddha, but a man can become a Buddha by the complete denial of the dual nature of self. Or rather, when a man has completely denied his duality, a Buddha appears. In order to realize Buddha in this way, one must follow the path of the historical Buddha – cast away all ties of this world – home, love, family – and live a pure, ascetic life. However, the act of casting away implies the existence of a self who casts away. Therefore the idea of casting away must be denied, that is, even denying must be denied. Then nothing remains of self, but this nothing is not non-existence; rather, it is a vivid continuing state.

Such a logic of double denial, a uniquely medieval way of thinking in Japan, came from the ascetic practices of Zen Buddhism, not from the application of logical thought. According to Zen, truth cannot be explained by words. Enlightenment comes from intuition gained through direct religious ascetic practices, not from any intellectual understanding or knowledge of written Buddhist doctrine, merely a finger pointing to the moon, but not the moon itself. At the crucial point of intuition one must cast away words, means, self and even the idea of casting away. At this moment there is no concept of a relative situation, no means or end, subject or object, beginning or ending, past or future. This moment embraces all of time; one is incorporated with all other Buddhas.

Thus words or writing were considered only one aid in approaching Buddhism; earth, mountains, rivers, wind, clouds – every kind of phenomenon – contained the potential to reveal Buddhist truth. Many medieval Zen gardens and paintings were an application of such thinking to artistic representations of Buddhism, symbols of the Buddhist cosmology. This concept of double denial influenced even such secular medieval artists as Zeami, and Bashō, analogous as it was to the creative experience of casting away preconceived notions to discover hidden truths.

Although Zen was part of the nucleus of Sung culture in China, medieval arts were not all symbols of Buddhist thought in Japan. Some poetry, 'sumie' – ink painting, dry gardens, etc. – directly followed secular Sung culture even when they were created by Zen priests. Zen thought – along with the ideas of other new sects of Buddhism – deeply influenced daily life in the turbulent Medieval Era, leading finally to the secularization of religion as in ancient times.

Traditional culture survived alongside the newly imported Sung culture in the form of 'waka' poems and such folk arts as 'sarugaku' plays, which originated in ancient primitive rites. 'Waka', 31-syllable poems, had been part of the cultural heritage of aristocratic society, but these ancient poems, vivid with life, and the symbolic court poetry had disappeared by the Middle Ages. However, a medieval poetic form called 'renga' developed from this tradition, which in turn led to the 'haiku' poem of seventeen syllables in which the symbolism and the delicacy of ancient court literature was revived. The 'haiku', as a form, was inextricably bound up with seasonal and natural symbolisms.

The 'wabi' and 'sabi' expressed in 'haiku' were a combination of the pessimism of the Jōdo sect of Buddhism and the self-denial of the Zen, reflected against the desolation of the wars of the period. This approach culminated in the tea ceremony of Riku and in the Haiku poems of Bashō.

The 'sarugaku' were performances of acrobatics and humorous mimes, some of which originated in early fertility rites. In the fourteenth century Kan'ami and his son Zeami transformed this traditional entertainment into the Nō-play to be performed with song and dance. The 'kuse-mai', the prototype of present Japanese dance, became very popular among the warriors and wealthy civilians. Thus the rise of the lower classes in medieval times led to the establishment of such popular arts as flower arrangement, while the shrine festivals lost their original religious significance, and became a purely secular form of entertainment.

The Feudal Period: the Culture of the Townsmen

Toyotomi Hideyoshi's control of both land and people at the end of the sixteenth century was both broader and stronger than that of the ancient Ritsuryō government. The Tokugawa military government which succeeded Hideyoshi built a new capital in Edo, and established a feudal system which would endure until 1868. The three centuries of the Tokugawa rule were generally peaceful, an era in which the warriors led the farmers, artisans and merchants both socially and administratively, but in reality the merchants became economically the most powerful group and, by the middle of the period, the most culturally creative. The population of the many towns which had been founded toward the end of the Medieval Period increased, and the merchants who controlled trade between the big cities of Kyōto, Osaka and Edo, and the rural districts, prospered.

The fundamental goal of Hideyoshi's agrarian policy had been to release the peasants from the complex chain of medieval land ownership and to guarantee the right of cultivation of individual holdings, though small, to each farmer. But the Tokugawa government, following its land survey of 1677, allowed tenant farming and the employment of laborers, whose names were ordered to be registered in the survey. The primary agricultural policy objective of the Tokugawa government was to increase the crop yields to support the ever increasing population. Moreover, as the peaceful period progressed, and the 'samurai' class became ever increasingly a bureaucratic class, and a parasitic, non-productive one, the increased tax yields of better crops became of greater concern.

From the beginning of the eighteenth century the feudal system began to decline, and affairs grew worse for every class except the merchants. Large scale land ownership–which was contrary to the basic principles of the feudal system–was revived as a result of the government's policy of encouraging wasteland reclamation. There was an increase in the number of idle warriors, especially those whose lords had been purged for some reason; for by law, these 'rōnin'–vagrant warriors–could not change their status to farmers, and so were not in a position easily to support themselves. The military talents which had once led Hideyoshi and Ieyasu to supreme power were unsuitable for administering the country in peacetime. Now the economic skills of the merchant class were paramount, but the warrior class, with its Confucian view of society which disdained commerce, despised the practice of these skills. Nevertheless, it followed the ostentatious and extravagant life style of the merchant class and was obliged to raise the tax from 40 per cent of the crop to 50 per cent and even 60 per cent in order to do so.

Meanwhile the merchants had become prosperous, and from the middle of the Edo Period they were the class which dominated the culture. This culture was basically amoral and distorted by the sense of social and political inferiority of the merchants.

During Hideyoshi's rule Ōsaka and Kyōto had been the centres of government and culture. The culture was patronized by the impoverished aristocrats and the influential merchants, who had participated in the traditional culture since the middle of the Medieval Period. Even after the government was transferred to Edo, both Kyōto and Ōsaka remained centres of culture where many schools of the various arts were established–'waka' and 'haiku', painting, calligraphy, Nō-drama, flower arrangement, the tea rituals, vocal and instrumental music, and even Chinese poetry. As they increased in popularity, most of these arts became formalized and lost their creative vitality; in contrast, Edo possessed no cultural tradition.

The most influential merchants were the dealers in cotton and lumber who were granted a privileged position in the new capital to stimulate commercial activity. They were invited from the native province of the Tokugawa family and from the Ōsaka-Kyōto area by the government.

In order to strengthen 'bakufu' control of the outlying areas the government instituted a system known as 'Sankin-Kōtai' requiring the 'daimyō' to maintain residences in Edo as well as in their home provinces, to spend alternate years–or half-years–in the capital, and to leave their wives and children there as hostages. The 'daimyō's' principal retainers remained at Edo with him. This created a shortage of women, since many of the retainers were forced to leave their families in the provinces, or were unmarried, and since many of the merchants' clerks were also single. To alleviate this enforced celibacy the government licensed the prostitution or gay quarter of Yoshiwara in 1617, and it was in this peculiar environment that Edo culture germinated. The guests of the gay quarter were warriors–and some of the feudal lords–who were still wealthy at this time, and the rich merchants and building contractors. Luxurious dissipation was the daily norm. Many beautiful young girls were brought to Yoshiwara from the villages, or from the impoverished upper class families of Kyōto, and were trained in the etiquette of the gay quarter, the arts of entertainment. The most accomplished were selected as 'tayū', the highest courtesans, and were the first ladies of both beauty and refinement, not only in the gay quarter but in the whole country. A kind of chivalry developed, in which the passionate senses were restrained and life regarded as a continual play; failure to abide by this code might cause tragedies for both courtesan and guest. Lovers committed suicide when they understood the reality of human love and its impossibility in the gay quarter, which was an idealized world of sex, not a real world of love.

Toward the middle of the Edo Period the life of the gay quarter gradually changed with the changing circumstances of the guests. The warriors' wealth was decreasing, while the smaller, non-privileged merchants who dealt directly in consumer goods were becoming wealthy. Luxurious dissipation by the speculative merchants and the highest courtesans came to an end, and there appeared other gay quarters for the middle class merchants and the artisans. The 'geisha' in these unlicensed gay quarters inherited the sense of play and the etiquette of Yoshiwara, and in due time established a new aesthetic called 'iki'.

'Iki', like 'wabi' in the Middle Ages, originated in the peculiar Japanese sensitivity to the environment: 'wabi' in the natural environment, and 'iki' in the social environment of the gay quarter, where most social intercourse took place in the later Edo Period. 'Iki' therefore developed as an aesthetic attitude with a strong sense of eroticism as its basis. However, mere coquetry to stimulate sexual feelings was not 'iki'; to be 'iki' required a sense of obstinacy or restraint, even if the intention was sexuality. Furthermore, 'iki' required a sense of resignation even when love was passionate; thus the feelings between sweethearts could not be 'iki'. An amorous overture was not 'iki'. These paradoxical definitions of the meaning of 'iki' have an affinity for the medieval logic of double denial, and both come from the psychological ambivalence of Japanese thought. If there was no sense of sexuality a situation could not be 'iki', yet the sexual act itself was definitely not 'iki'. Its sphere lay somewhere between these two poles, mixed with feelings of stoic suppression and obstinate resistance which reflected the mental state of the merchants of this time, who enjoyed wealth but were socially and politically suppressed. A simple example of the artistic expression of 'iki' was the figure of a woman wearing the informal cotton 'kimono', the 'yukata', after taking a bath. To express 'iki', special facial expressions, shape of body, posture, pattern of the cloth and gestures were important. The sense of warmth from the bath was appreciated; the same figure without taking a bath, or nude, or wearing formal clothes, was not 'iki'.

From the middle of the Edo Period this peculiar and subtle aesthetic was expressed in 'ukiyo-e', wood block prints, 'shamisen' music, 'kabuki' drama and some literature. In a sense these were decadent arts, neither healthy nor intellectual, since the townsmen were not intellectual, nor did they live the healthy open-air life of the peasant, yet compared to the traditional and conventionalized arts of 'waka' and 'haiku' poetry, 'Nō'-plays and other of the older forms as practised in the Edo Period generally, the 'iki' art forms were vivid and creative.

The first Europeans to arrive in Japan appear to have been shipwrecked Portuguese, who brought the first firearms, in 1543. Six years later, St. Francis Xavier arrived and founded his mission. However, the efforts of the missionaries lasted for only eighty years. In 1635, travel abroad by Japanese was forbidden by the government, and after 1639, all foreigners were expelled, except Dutch traders permitted to live for the next two centuries on Deshima, a small artificial island in Nagasaki Bay. Perhaps the most important impact of the Dutch presence was the gradual introduction to Japan, in the eighteenth and nineteenth centuries of the sciences and rational thought of contemporary Europe. However, the 'Rangakusha', the scholars of Western learning, were harassed and suppressed, and many of them imprisoned, throughout the period.

From the middle of the Edo Period successive famines threatened the peasants' livelihood, causing riots in the towns and the country. The need to reform the government was felt by many intelligent men, especially after capricious laws were passed by the government as an attempt at reform. In the western provinces, far from the luxurious and extravagant cities, the middle and lower classes improved their social positions through provincial and private school education, and prospered. These newly educated men, low ranking 'samurai', were the driving force in the overthrow of the Tokugawa warrior's government which was replaced by the imperial restoration in 1867.

Plates

Hōryū-ji (Nara Prefecture)

55 In the foreground, the central gate, the pagoda, the central hall, and the assembly hall. On both sides are the buildings for the sutras and the bell.

56 From the left, the Kondō, the Chūmon, and the pagoda. All three buildings as well as the roofed walks are of the Asuka Style. These are the oldest Buddhist buildings in Japan, built 1200 years ago.

57 The covered passage, Kwairō. The posts have entasis.

58 Pagoda, about 105′ high. The eaves of the second and fourth roofs are not aligned with the eaves of the first, third and fifth roofs, but are set back from them.

59 Chūmon. The use of an even number of bays in an entrance gate is very rare.

60 Tō-in, the eastern precinct of Hōryū-ji. During the seventh century, Prince Shōtoku's residence was in this precinct. The octagonal Yume-dono was dedicated to the prince a century later. The monumental structure was surrounded by corridors, with a gate house. The buildings were repaired and rebuilt in the eighth and thirteenth centuries.

61 Detail of the octagonal roof.

62 Interior of the Kondō. The image of the Shakyamuni Buddha is in Asuka Style, the oldest sculptural style native to Japan.

63 The interior of the Yume-dono, with the statue of the priest Gyōshin, its founder.

Tōshōdai-ji (Nara Prefecture)

64 The larger building is the Kondō; the Kōdō is to the left.

65 Kondō, the Main Hall. This massive building in the style of the T'ang dynasty was constructed by the Chinese priest Ch'ien-chen.

66 The front colonnade of the Kondō.

67 The interior of the Kondō.

Murō-ji (Nara Prefecture)

68 The Kondō, as seen from the foot of the stone steps. This temple of the Shingon Sect was founded in 681 A.D. by the priest En-no-Shōkaku, although the current structure dates from the 9th century.

69 Kondō. The veranda façade is an addition of Edo Period.

70 The side of the Kondō, showing the bays which formed the original Heian period hall.

71 The Pagoda. 43′ high, 8′ square in plan. Miniature scale and exquisite colours give the Murō-ji pagoda more the feeling of a toy than of a piece of architecture.

Hōō-dō, Byōdō-in, Uji (Kyōto Prefecture)

72 The Phoenix Hall.

73 The façade of the Hōō-dō is modeled after the Palace of the Buddha, in the Pure Land, as it appears in a Jōdo 'mandala'.

74 Interior, showing the elaborately coloured ceiling.

Tōshōgū, Nikkō (Tochigi Prefecture)

75 Ō-torii, the first gate, and Omote-mon, the formal entrance gate. The central part of the shrine has the usual symetrical plan but the overall plan resembles that of a castle, because of the still turbulent situation in the country and the topography of the site.

76 Yōmei-mon, the middle gate.

77 Shinko, the storehouse for sacred objects, and the Yōmei-mon.

78 Kara-mon, the inner gate, and the Hall of Worship. Gilding and metal-work on a white background decorate the attached roofed fence.

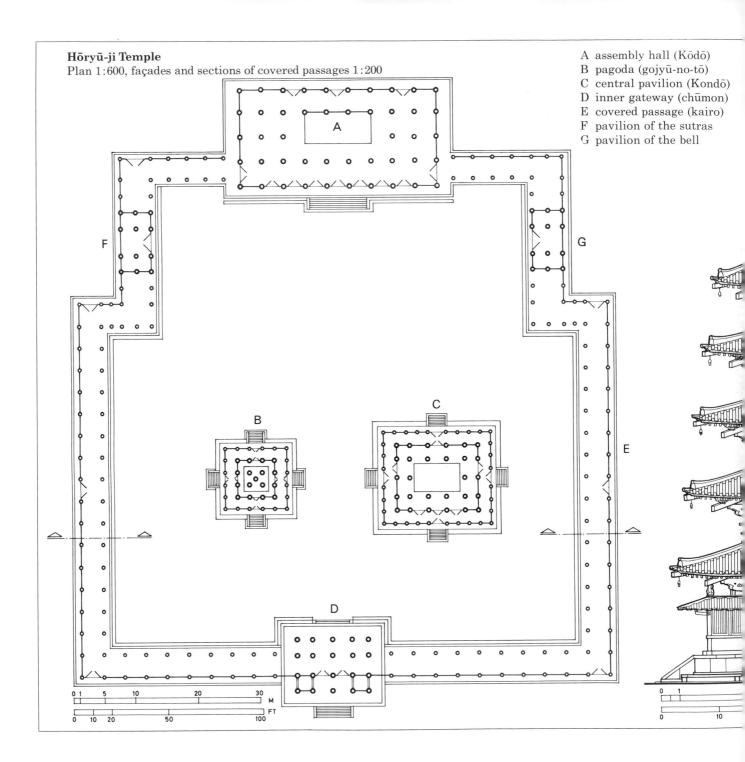

Hōryū-ji Temple
Plan 1:600, façades and sections of covered passages 1:200

A assembly hall (Kōdō)
B pagoda (gojyū-no-tō)
C central pavilion (Kondō)
D inner gateway (chūmon)
E covered passage (kairo)
F pavilion of the sutras
G pavilion of the bell

A

F

G

B

C

E

D

0 1 5 10 20 30 M
0 10 20 50 100 FT

0 1 10

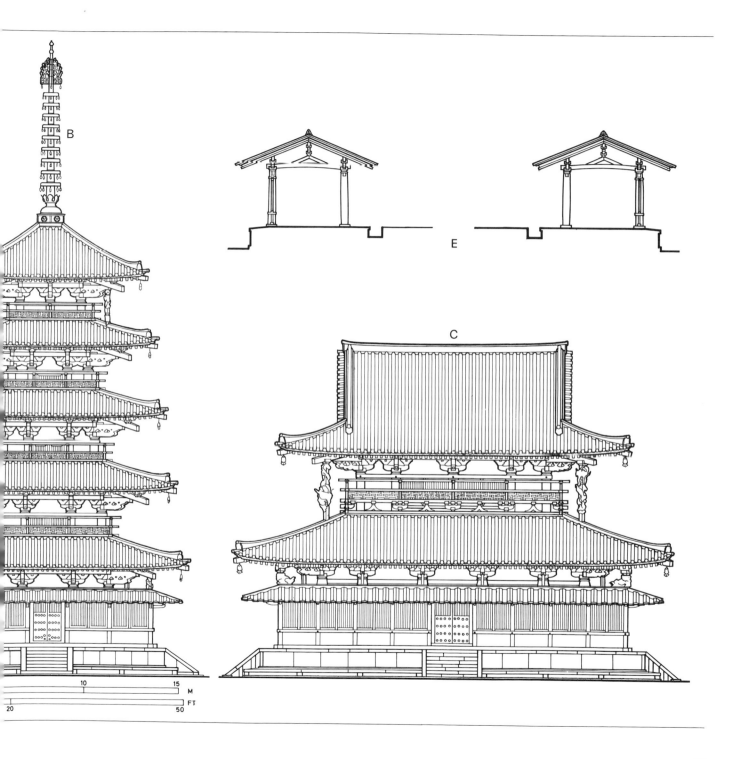

B

E

C

10   15
M
20   50 FT

Notes

Hōryū-ji and its Style

The 'Nihon-Shoki', the 'Official Chronicle of Japan', records that Hōryū-ji was struck by lightning, and completely destroyed by fire, in April of the year 670. However, the official report presented to the government by the temple in 731 listed all the principal edifices, with the exception of the Kō-dō, and made no reference to the fire. The same report listed the images of the Buddhist guardian dieties flanking the Chū-mon, or entrance gate, as having been produced between 708 and 714.

In 1939, the remains of an ancient temple were discovered in the precincts of Hōryū-ji, and were identified as the ruins of the original temple. The extant Hōryū-ji is therefore a product of the years from 670 to 714, a period of great significance in the history of Japanese architecture. It was in this period that the Imperial Ise Shrine was founded, and the Yakushi-ji temple was completed in the Asuka District. Yakushi-ji was later transferred to its present site in Nara. Each of these groupings was in a different style.

Many of the priests at Hōryū-ji in the seventh century were from the Korean kingdom of Paekche. According to a bronze inscription of the period, many of them left the temple after the fire. The Kudara Kannon, a Paekche image of the bodhisattva, is exemplary of the strange and somewhat alien feeling of all the buildings in the complex. In fact, the buildings were constructed using the Korean 'koma-shaku' measuring unit, and we may suppose that the reconstruction was undertaken by carpenters and refugee priests from Paekche, or that at the very least they had trained the builders.

The main buildings of Hōryū-ji, the pagoda of Yakushi-ji, and the main hall of Tōshōdai-ji, are representative examples of the architecture of the Asuka, Hakuhō, and Tempyō periods, respectively. The main hall of Tōshōdai-ji was designed by the Chinese Buddhist priest, Ch'ien-chen.

The Scene of the Pure Land: The Phoenix Hall of the Byōdō-in

The Jōdo – Pure Land – Sect of Buddhism, at the end of the Heian Period, was a flight from the reality of death in a melancholy mood. The priest Enshin (942–1017) preached that the experience of the moment was experience of the final moment of the world. The believer's fervent wish for salvation at the instant of death, is of greater value than 100 years' daily religious training. The believer who places total faith in Salvation through the strength of the Amitabha Buddha will, at the instant of his death, be reborn in the Pure Land – Paradise. He who is saved shall be reborn on a lotus flower, in the Pond of Mercy in the Pure Land.

All about the Pond of Mercy bloom wondrous flowers, each a jewel of different hue. The blues and yellows sparkle, the reds and whites vibrate intensely, and all tremble gently in the slightest breezes.

The palaces and the lofty pavilions of varied jewels, the fragrant trees, the singing birds, the celestial angels playing music, the people reborn, the bodhisattvas, and Amitabha complete the magnificent, brilliant and colorful scene of the Pure Land.

These ideas were realized in the Hoō-dō of Byōdō-in, especially in ceremonial occasions of the past.

On Tōshō-gū

The architectural forms of Tōshō-gū and Katsura Villa represent the two extremes of Japanese architecture, and resulted from the extreme difference in taste between the powerful, newly established, warrior class and the declining aristocratic culture. This difference is similar to that between the castle and the tea room in a previous era, which represented the social tension between the warriors and the merchants. Thus Tōshō-gū was a monument to the triumph of the warriors over two cultures or social classes; later, from the middle of the Edo Period, the ascendancy of the warrior class was gradually reversed by the tenacious rise of the merchants.

Tōshō-gū was at first constructed in Sumpu, Shizuoka Prefecture, and was transferred in 1617 to its present site on Futara Mountain, which had been a sacred mountain since the earliest times. Tōshō-gū was reconstructed 18 years later on the order of the third Tokugawa Shōgun. The existing building resulted from the modification of the roofs 20 years later, in the most authoritative period of the three centuries of Edo Government.

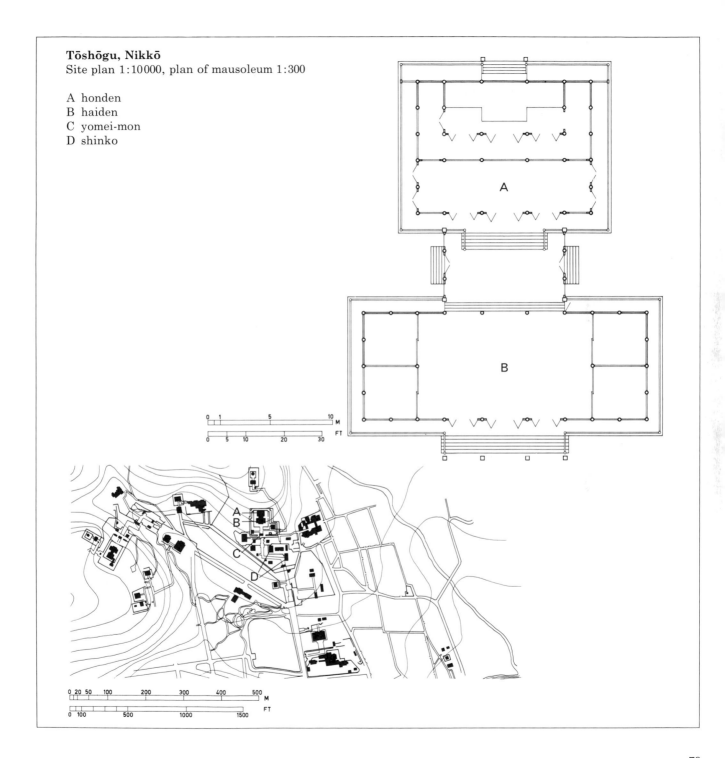

Tōshōgu, Nikkō
Site plan 1:10000, plan of mausoleum 1:300

A honden
B haiden
C yomei-mon
D shinko

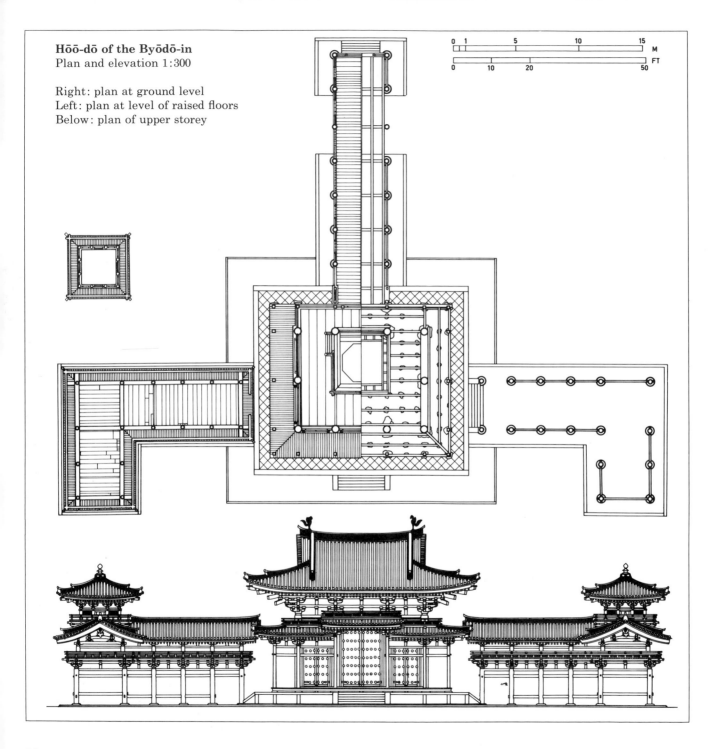

Hōō-dō of the Byōdō-in
Plan and elevation 1:300

Right: plan at ground level
Left: plan at level of raised floors
Below: plan of upper storey

2. History of Architecture

The Burial Mound

Many songs and poems, especially the elegies in the classical anthologies, express the empathy of the ancient people for the mountain. They attributed animistic spirits to mountains of unique shape or scale, and believed them to be the place where the soul of the dead departed from the earth to hang forever in the sky.

The ancient burial mound, 'kofun', was called 'yama'–hill, or mountain–in ancient times, which suggests an association of the mounds with mountains. The 'Wei Shih', a third century Chinese history, makes reference to the custom of burying the dead in either the mountains or the forests, and recommends this the practice rather than the construction of tree covered burial mounds. It would thus appear that both practices were current at that time. The 'Wei Shih' had been brought to Japan, but the connection, if any, between the burial mounds in Japan and customs on the mainland is not clear.

The earliest type of 'kofun' of the third and fourth centuries were actual hills excavated to form a high, round mound, joined to a low rectangular platform for a ritual performance. There are no records of the burial rite itself.

A canoe-shaped wooden coffin, made from a large natural log, from sixteen to twenty feet long, was placed on a beaten clay floor in a vertical pit in the centre of the mound, nearly level with the ritual platform. The walls of the pit were lined with stone slabs; bronze mirrors both native and imported, third century Wei Dynasty products, swords, jewels and spear heads were arranged close to the coffin. The burial chamber was roofed with flat stone slabs grouted with a mixture of clay and gravel, then covered with a thick layer of clay. The whole surface of the mound was usually faced with small stones and was sometimes encircled by several rows of clay tubes, to prevent the soil being washed away in heavy rains. The planting of trees on the mound probably was for the same purpose. These mounds, as most mounds in Japan, were constructed by an artisans' guild called the 'haji-be'.

In the fifth century the scale and siting of the

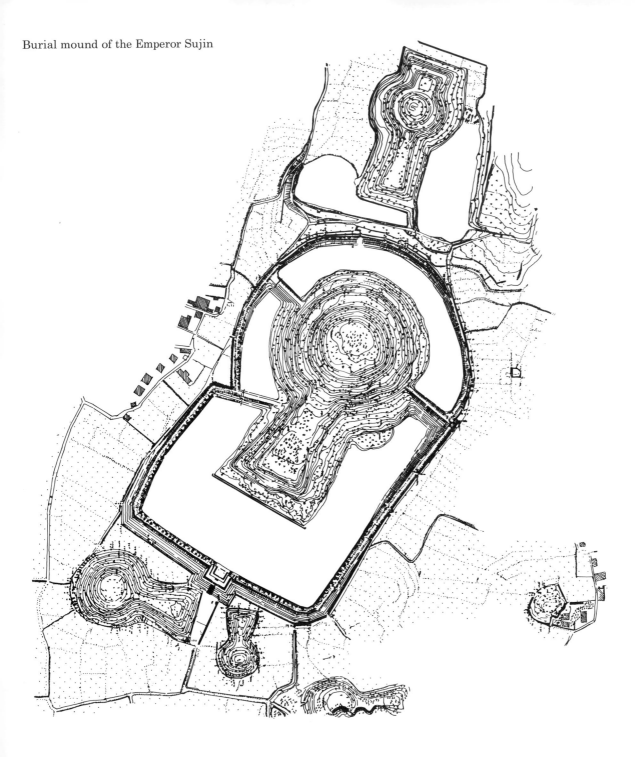

Burial mound of the Emperor Sujin

mounds changed. Magnificent mounds were constructed such as those for the Emperors Nintoku and Ōjin. The mounds were now built in the low highlands and later in the alluvial plains. The earth excavated from the surrounding moat was used to form the mound. The ritual platform became trapezoidal and the same height as the mound, the whole plan resembling a keyhole. The mound was faced with stone as before, but rows of clay models, figurines of houses, umbrellas, etc., replaced the simple tubes. The wooden coffin was sometimes no longer enclosed in a chamber but completely covered with clay. Later the wooden coffin was replaced by a stone one of the same type or a cist placed in the chamber; later there appeared house-shaped cists.

In the sixth and seventh centuries a different type of burial chamber appears; previously the pits had

Gobyōyama burial mound

been excavated vertically but now the megalithic chamber was approached horizontally. It became a room lined with huge stones, with an inclined passage leading to a stone door. Both the chamber and the passage were buried in the mound.

The objects buried with the body changed from the weapons, arms, and other ritual utensils of former times to saddles and bridles for horses, and everyday cooking utensils. This new type of mound usually had either a round or square plan, and its form was an imitation of burial mounds in China. The idea of the after world also seems to have changed from heaven to an underground world.

The collective passionate act of making such huge burial mounds ended with the Imperial Edict of A.D. 646 prohibiting their construction, and with the introduction of the Buddhist rite of cremation these energies were channelled into the construction of temples.

The Shrine

'Chi', 'ke', 'tama', and 'mono', aspects of the spirit recorded in the early Japanese classics – the 'Kojiki' (A.D. 712) and the 'Nihongi' of the 'Nihonshoki' (A.D. 720) – are animatic, while some others are animistic. People were afraid even to name these spirits, since the word itself had a spirit, 'koto-dama', and such beliefs, though they have changed slightly, are still expressed in certain magic religious ceremonies practiced today.

Sacred articles or vessels used for worshipping them were kept in a sacred place or store. The 'Fudoki', a classic geographic text, recorded sacred rockseats, 'iwakura', some of which have been excavated by archaeologists, revealing sacred objects such as swords or bells. On Oki Island in the Korean Strait there is an extant example of a sacred natural storage place, where consecrated relics are housed in the shadow of sacred rocks, 'iwakage'. At Ise and Suwa Shrines there are sacred rocks, and sacred stones kept in shrines, and sacred man-made posts – 'hashira' – as a symbol of haunting spirits.

These spirits, or forces, were anthropomorphized in the classics as 'kami', Japanese gods. They were included in the hierarchy of the Imperial family's ancestor goddess, Amaterasu, but the history of their original personification and birthplace is not recorded.

Generally a fertility spirit became the god of a particular district and the guardian god of a particular family or families dwelling there. Originally each small district probably had a god with a special name, sacred place, and ceremonies, but as dense settlements grew around the rice cultivation areas, and as political unity was achieved in the Yayoi Period, these gods became merged and unified. The gods called 'Suwa-no-kami' and 'Ise-no-kami' in the classics have several names and we may thus infer the political unity of several different gods.

When a god is anthropomorphized he needs a dwelling. The sacred rock, seats of Ō-omiwa Shrine, the sacred enclosure – 'himorogi' – mentioned in the classics, and the 'shin-no-mihashira' – sacred central pillar – at Ise shrine were sanctuaries for the personified god who had lived there since protohistoric times.

We can trace the development of this dwelling from a temporary to a permanent shrine from the rituals recorded in the classics. At Izumo the goddess dwelt in a mound piled with boughs, and at Kamo the 'miare' ritual symbolized the coming of the god. At Kamo the priestess waited for the god to appear beside a sacred enclosure built with boughs containing a sacred branch, the 'miare-gi'. At Daijō-kyū a temporary shrine was erected for the 'Niiname', the primitive communion. The emperor secretly communed with the Rice Spirit to ensure long life and the fertility of the crops. The Sumiyoshi Shrine is one of the most primitive examples of a permanent shrine, being similar to the plan type of the shrine at Daijō-kyū.

Ise Shrine is a fusion of several concepts: the sacred storage of a holy mirror, the dwelling of the sun goddess, the ancestral shrine of the Imperial family, and the dwelling of the district god of Ise, symbolized in the central pillar under the shrine. Because of its connection with the Imperial family and the nation it has become the archetypal shrine.

It is possible to reconstruct the original Ise Shrine on the basis of historical restorations of the Takara-

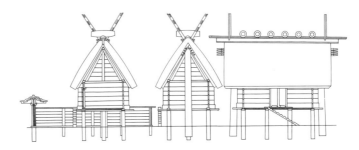

Main building of the Aramatsuri-no-miya, one of the secondary shrines at Ise (after Fukuyama): section, lateral façade, main façade

den, or sacred treasure house, the Mike-den, the hall of sacred meals, both in the holy enclosure at Ise, and the 'Aramatsuri-no-miya', shrine of the active spirit of the god of Ise, which houses another holy mirror. Reconstructing from these sources, the original buildings at Ise appear to have used horizontal planks overlapping at the corners in the prehistoric 'azekura' style of the grain warehouses. But this construction resulted in a building too small for an important national shrine, and it was enlarged by employing free-standing ridgeposts to support the ridgepole. Later the shrine was further enlarged using post and beam construction, as seen at Ise today. Such changes in shrine design probably correspond to the evolution of the god from the spirit to the human ancestor.

To symbolize the holiness of the shrine it must be built in a traditionally holy place, the area tabooed, isolated from the secular world by deep forests, mountains or water. Above all, the classics and ancient prayers demand a grand and awesome building.

The style of the central shrine of present day Ise is called 'Shimmei zukuri', and those buildings which have a ridgepost free-standing outside the end walls are called 'Yuiitsu-shimmei zukuri', unique 'Shimmei zukuri'. A shrine with the same plan but with one side of the roof extended to cover the entrance stair is called 'Nagare zukuri'. This extension was most probably dictated by the needs of offerings and other rituals. At Usa Hachiman Shrine in Kyūshū, 'Hachiman zukuri', and Hiyoshi Shrine in Shiga Prefecture,

The different styles of Shinto shrines

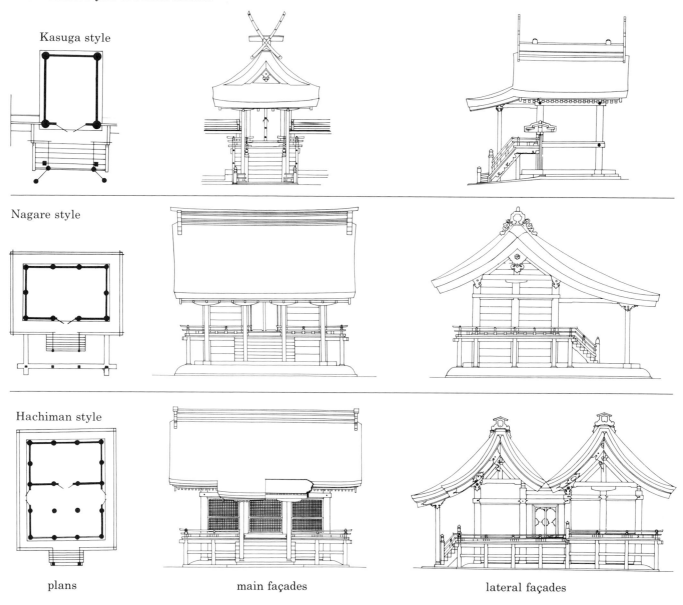

Kasuga style

Nagare style

Hachiman style

plans   main façades   lateral façades

'Hie zukuri', and most specifically at the Kibitsu Shrine in Okayama Prefecture, this need for a ritual space developed to include a prayer room for par-

ticipants in front of the sanctuary, and stimulated the construction of a separate hall of worship, as in Buddhist temples. In some cases an ancestral god and a guardian Buddha were included in the same hall with the worshipper. It will be shown later that this secularization of the sacred shrine led to the use of the residential style called 'Shinden zukuri' at such shrines as Itsukushima and others. The Kitano Shrine is composed of three parts: the sanctuary, the hall of worship, and a link between them where the priests prayed. The complex roof which covers these three spaces is the prototype of the style called 'Gongen zukuri', of which the shrine at Nikkō is an example.

Most shrines in Japan are constructed in one of these styles, all of which are based on the Ise prototype; important exceptions are the smaller Kasuga Shrine, 'Kasuga zukuri', and the larger Izumo Shrine, 'Taisha zukuri', which both have their entrances at the gable end of the building, similar to the Sumiyoshi Shrine. In the Kasuga Shrine, the sanctuary is a small chamber with a centrally placed entrance stair, whereas at Izumo the stair is eccentric. The most notable difference between Kasuga and the 'Shimmei zukuri' is the roof construction. At both Ise and Izumo the stair was originally uncovered, and later an inclined board roof of rather temporary nature was added, but at Kasuga the main roof was extended to form a hipped end over the entrance stair.

Kasuga Shrine is unique not only in its roof construction, but also in its painting, which is stylistically that of a Buddhist temple. These differences are probably explained by its origin as a tutelary shrine for the Fujiwara family, a powerful clan in the ancient period, exceeding even the emperor in authority. They chose its site in the new capital of Nara, whereas the sites of Ise and Kamo were prehistoric holy places of animistic worship, isolated from populated areas. In contrast to the small sanctuary in the Kasuga Shrine, there is a two-storied entrance gate connected to a beautiful covered walkway, similar to the Kamo Shrine.

There are several types of shrine precinct. Kitano Shrine has a courtyard, enclosed by covered walks connected to a two storied entrance gate at the front, and the ritual hall at the rear. The sanctuary is outside the courtyard at the back of the ritual hall. Another shrine has a hall for sacred dances in the centre of its courtyard. The Iwashimizu Shrine has a similar courtyard, with the sanctuary at the centre of the courtyard where Kitano Shrine's hall of sacred dances is located. Other shrines have only a sanctuary and an independent hall of worship.

The hall of worship and the covered ways were both used by the participants in the ceremonies, and the shrines came to be the centre of community life. Only the priests were admitted to the ritual hall. The roofed gate, corresponding to the 'torii' at Ise, a simple post and beam gate which marked the ceremonial entrance to the sacred enclosure, was established under the influence of Buddhist temple architecture.

Until quite recently, most shrines were constructed in the traditional manner. Despite the identification of Shintō gods with Buddhas in the latter half of the ancient period, and the changes in Shintō ritual in the Middle Ages, there was little change in the architectural style of the shrine. But when the worship of national heroes such as Toyotomi Hideyoshi and Tokugawa Ieyasu was instituted in the feudal period, richly decorated sanctuaries filled with coloured carvings were erected in their honor. The shrines were even more grandiose than their own 'Shoin zukuri' residential style of the sixteenth and seventeenth centuries. However, their plan type is based on the ancient tradition; their most important development was in the complex shape of the roof, as in the 'Gongen zukuri' roofs of Tōshōgū, Ieyasu's tomb at Nikkō.

The Buddhist Temple

The introduction of Buddhism ended the construction of huge burial mounds. In the Taika Edict, in 645, local magnates were forbidden to build burial mounds, and cremation was recommended, in accordance with Buddhist belief. Before this time the erection of Buddhist temples had been introduced by Chinese and Korean immigrants who became naturalized Japanese, and temple construction had also become popular with such local magnates as the Soga family.

In 588, the construction of Asuka-dera, or Hōkō-ji, was decreed, and in that year six monks and carpen-

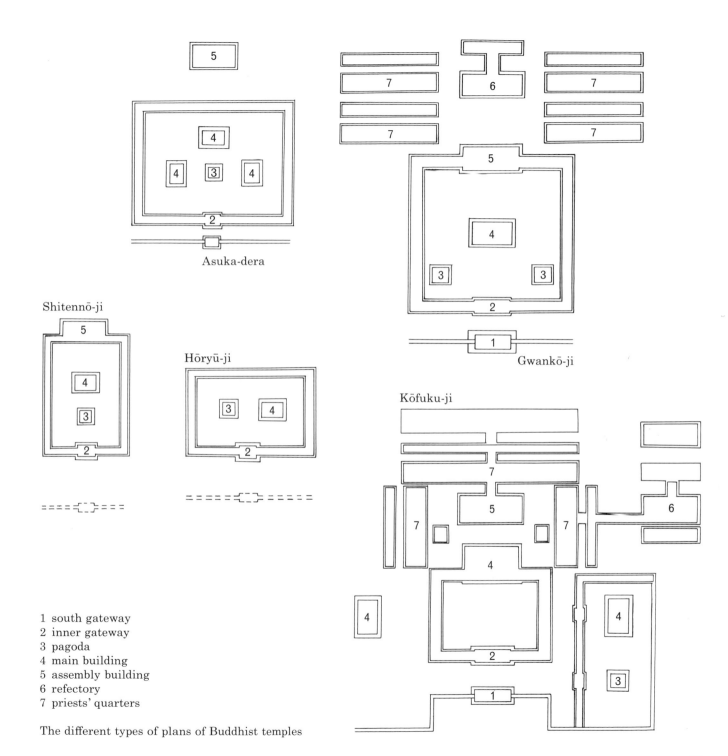

Asuka-dera

Shitennō-ji

Hōryū-ji

Gwankō-ji

Kōfuku-ji

1 south gateway
2 inner gateway
3 pagoda
4 main building
5 assembly building
6 refectory
7 priests' quarters

The different types of plans of Buddhist temples

ters, smiths, roof-tile makers and other experts in temple construction were invited to Japan from Paekche, one of the three ancient Korean kingdoms. It is probable that they were employed in the construction of this temple, since archaeological excavations show that the plan of the temple precinct, which is no longer extant, was based on precedents in Paekche. Four years later construction work was started, and in 593, the first year of the reign of the Empress Suiko, a jewel symbolic of the sacred bone of Shakyamuni, the historical Buddha, was installed at the foot of the central post of the pagoda. Three years later, in 596, the pagoda was completed, and in 606 the principle Buddha image was installed in the main central hall, Chū-kondō. The complete construction required nearly twenty years. In the eastern main hall, the Tō-kondō, a stone image of Miroku (the Bodhisattva Maitreya) was enshrined which had been imported from Paekche in 584.

The construction of Shitennōji Temple in Naniwa, the present Ōsaka, was begun in 593, and that of Ikaruga-dera in the western part of Yamato, about 606. The arrangements of the precincts of these temples were different from Asuka-dera, but they were also based on precedents in Paekche.

Hōryū-ji in the south-west section of Nara and adjacent to Ikaruga-dera, was completed about one century later. It has an unusual asymmetrical precinct plan, which probably resulted from the restrictions of the site. However, as the Japanese have shown an indifference to strict symmetry, which was the symbol of eternity, it is probably also an early example of this disposition.

When the capital was moved to Nara in 710, the most important temples from the Asuka district were also transferred, among them the remaining eastern pagoda of Yakushi-ji. Private temples also transferred included Kōfuku-ji belonging to the Fujiwara family, which was enlarged on this occasion, and Asuka-dera, later called Gankō-ji, which belonged to the Soga family. The eastern end of the capital was enlarged to provide sites for these temples, resulting in an asymmetrical city plan quite different from the original model in T'ang China.

The most important new temple constructed at Nara was Tōdai-ji, as the central temple of the nation, and each of the sixty-four provinces were ordered to construct provincial temples, both for priests and nuns, and to install the image of Shakyamuni as the principle Buddha image. Many of their remains still exist. The purpose of these temples was to place the nation under the protection of Shakyamuni. Despite this edict the principle image which was finally enshrined at the central temple, Tōdai-ji, was not Shakyamuni but Vairocana, the Buddha of the Ideal World. Thus Buddhism had moved from the political idea of a guardian god to an interest in realizing the Ideal World, either in this life or the next. According to the Edict these temples were to be the flower of the country, their sites to be selected with the aim of separating the temple from the secular world, while at the same time keeping them close enough to settlements for the convenience of the believers. It is interesting to compare this idea with the choice of site of the later esoteric schools of tantric Buddhism such as the Tendai and Shingon sects of the Heian Period, and of the later Zen sect of the Middle Ages, most of which were hidden deep in the mountains. Other schools such as the Shinshū and Hokkeshū sects, whose priests preached in the towns and villages, were situated closer to settled areas.

The relationship between Buddhism and politics put political power into the hands of the priests, who finally came to dominate the court at the end of the Nara Period. The capital was therefore removed from Nara to Nagaoka and then to Heian-kyō, the present day Kyōto.

The six sects of Buddhism in Nara had only studied doctrinal Buddhism, and had no connection with the common people. They were parasites of the aristocracy. The newly imported Tendai and Shingon schools of the early Heian Period practiced a doctrine of ascetism in their mountain retreats. One school which attained religious ecstasy through the musical chanting of the name of Amitabha Buddha fused with the Jōdo sect which taught the people of the existence of a Buddhist paradise, or Pure Land.

All these new sects naturally brought about changes in the architectural style: the temple precincts of the esoteric schools, because of their remote moun-

Plans of the main buildings of Buddhist monasteries

a) Kondō of the Tōshōdai-ji, Nara (about the 8th c.)
b) Hondō of the Jōruri-ji, Kyōto (1107)
c) Hokkedō of the Tōdai-ji, Nara (about 748). The hall of
   worship (1199)
d) Konpon-chū-dō of the Enryaku-ji, near Kyōto (plan-type
   of the 10th c.)
e) Hondō of the Daihoon-ji, Kyōto (1227)
f) Hondō of the Honren-ji, Okayama (1492)

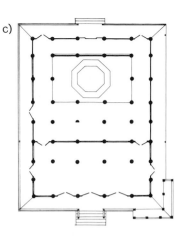

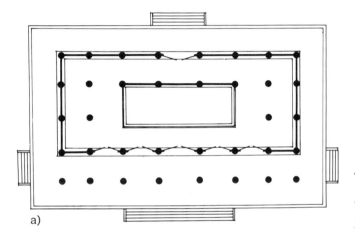

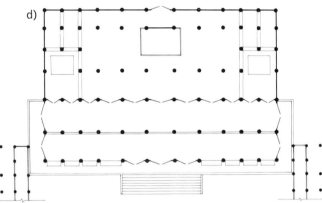

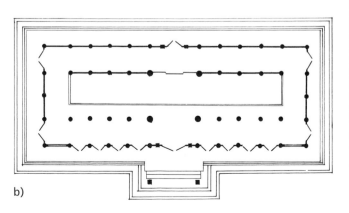

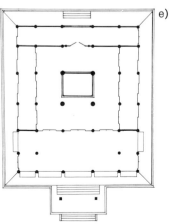

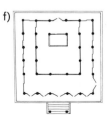

tain sites, were no longer symmetrical or formal as were the ancient temples of Nara and Asuka, and the spatial organization in individual buildings also changed with the changing rituals. The ancient temple housed only the Buddha image, which was worshipped from the courtyard. This courtyard was separated from the secular world by covered ways, which formed the courtyard wall. Inside the temple of the esoteric schools was a place for the priests, who performed rituals of burning homa-wood to destroy earthly desires by the flame of the Buddha's wisdom, chanting the name of Amitabha and contemplating his image, making secret hand gestures, and worshipping offerings. These rituals were performed before a hanging scroll, a 'mandala' depicting scenes of the enlightenment of Buddha. Followers were not admitted to these secret rituals, but prayed in the front chamber, partly screened from the inner sanctum with its mystic atmosphere of flickering lights, the sound of chanting, prayer gongs, and the smell of incense. The places of ritual and worship had been combined under one roof, making it possible to locate these temples in the mountains, there being now no need for an enclosed courtyard. The worshippers became participants in the world of Buddha, and this experience of an esoteric, symbolic atmosphere, combined with the idea of the Pure Land of the Jōdo sects, the traditional animistic appreciation of the natural landscape, and the new Zen concept of natural landscape, produced the various spatial expressions of the Medieval Period.

Murō-ji was a mountain temple of the Shingon school. The five story pagoda and the main hall, the Kondō, were constructed in the eighth century. Except for the front part of the main hall which is a later addition, the form of its main part remains that of the early esoteric temples. The pagoda is also an example of the same sect of Buddhism as is the tenth century five story pagoda of Daigo-ji.

A temple form of the ninth century called 'Jōgyō-dō' had an image of Amitabha Buddha enshrined in the centre of the hall. The interior walls were covered with murals, most of which depicted the Pure Land, and the worshippers proceeded around the image reciting the name of Amitabha. This ritual

guaranteed salvation in Paradise. As the Jōdo sect became popular, the interior of the main hall, called the 'Amidadō', the Hall of Amitabha, was embellished with opulent sculptures, paintings and religious vessels which eventually became more important than the ritual itself. These art forms, had a mystical and melancholic beauty which was the ideal of the then decadent Heian court culture.

In the tenth and eleventh centuries the Fujiwara family and the ex-emperors, hoping to gain paradise, constructed many private temples of which the Phoenix Hall, the Hōō-dō of the Byōdō-in, is an example. This was an Amitabha Hall dedicated by the Kampaku, Fujiwara Yorimichi, and built at his villa at Uji, which had belonged to his father, Michinaga. The villa is no longer extant. People of the time said: If doubtful of paradise, pay your respects at Uji. The hall is a representation of a palace in the Buddhist Paradise, as it appears in the 'mandalas', and is a typical example of the art of the Jōdo school. Though it had imitations, none now exist.

As the rituals of the Tendai and Shingon sects became prayers and incantations for recovery from illness, achievement, profit or other secular motives, these performances became daily practices in the aristocrats' residences in front of a temporary arrangement for worship. In the thirteenth century imperial villas for ex-emperors and residences for aristocrats, combined with a permanent Buddha Hall, were built outside the Heian capital at scenic hillside sites. This combination of residence and Buddha Hall is called 'Mido-gosho', and the architectural style of the Buddha Hall was adopted as the residential style, the 'Shinden zukuri'. Thus religion became a part of daily life, and the pilgrimage to the temple became a kind of amusement.

Among the many temples dedicated by emperors, the only remaining example of the golden age of 'Insei' is the 'Sanjusangen-dō', the Hall of Thirty-three Bays. It was reconstructed in 1266, a century after its consecration.

Both the declining aristocracy and the rising warrior class had a growing wish for rebirth in paradise in the turbulent days in the latter half of the twelfth century. This wish was reinforced by the belief that

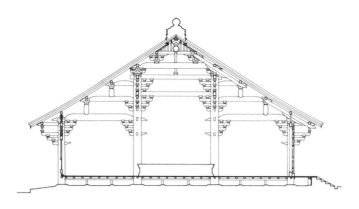

Jyōdo-dō of the Jyōdo-ji (Tōdai-ji style): transverse section

the age of salvation by Buddhism was coming to an end. Those who could afford to erected Amitabha Halls and looked to Amitabha Buddha for salvation, not through the expiation of sins through piety, but by the mere dedication of material wealth. This fashion spread widely, even to regions far from the capital. Several existing Amitabha Halls of that period, Chūson-ji in Iwate Prefecture, Jōruri-ji to the south in Kyōto, Hōkai-ji to the east of Kyōto, and Sanzen-in, to the north of Kyōto, are examples of this trend. In these Amitabha Halls the plan had evolved to provide a space for worship either in front of or surrounding the image.

Structural techniques had also developed in the preceding periods, producing a double roof structure system in which the true structure was hidden above an imitation structure under the eaves, which followed and reproduced the details of the true structure.

In the last decade of the twelfth century, Minamoto no Yoritomo overthrew the last vestiges of the 'Insei' System, and established a 'bakufu' or military government at Kamakura. It was at about this time that two new architectural styles were imported from the Southern Sung with the Zen school of Buddhism. One was called the 'Zenshū' style or 'kara-yō'; the other was called 'Tenjiku-yō', or 'Daibutsu'–great Buddha image–style, a style best represented at the Tōdai-ji in Nara. The 'Daibutsu' style was imported by a single

priest and survived only for a period of twenty years, but it was used in several important buildings, including the reconstruction of Tōdai-ji. The style was named after this building. The traditional Japanese style became known as 'wa-yō'. Gradually the distinctions among the three styles became blurred and, in later buildings, details of all three were combined.

The characteristics of 'Zenshū-yō' were: general slenderness of the structural members, columns tapering at both ends and supported on a wooden baseboard, decorative use of many timber blocks and brackets, 'masu-gumi', and radiating rafters under the eaves, flat wooden ceilings, use of a special type of window, 'Katō-mado', and framed doors, 'Sankarato'. The traditional 'wa-yō' door was a flush door of thick wooden boards. The plan-type of the temple precinct of the Zen school also differed radically from the traditional one because of its different function. The Zen temple was used by a priestly group

Shariden of the Enkaku-ji (Zen style): transverse section

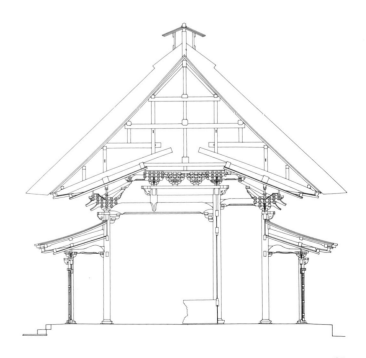

practising a formalized ascetic life within the precinct. The arrangement of buildings of one sect of Zen, the Rinzai sect, originally followed the Chinese precedent exactly. The Buddhist gate, the 'Sanmon', the central hall enshrining the Buddha Shakya-muni, the 'Butsuden', and the assembly hall, the 'Hattō', were placed inside the courtyard on axis, and linked by covered walks. To the sides in front of the courtyard were the lavatories, 'tōsu', and bathrooms, 'yoku-tō'. Outside the courtyard on both sides were the priests' apartments, 'sōdō', and stores, 'kōin', and behind the courtyard were the guesthouse, 'shuryō', and the chief priests' private quarters, 'hōjō', with gardens. Later the way of life of the Zen priests changed, resulting in the reorganization of the precinct, and 'hōjō' came to mean the priests' living quarters combined with a small temple, and arranged around the compound, as at Daitokuji in Kyōto.

The 'Daibutsu-yō' was characterized by the use of many horizontal members bracing the columns, giving a great feeling of strength, the use of a unique form of block and bracket, and the absence of a ceiling. Both the Jōdo-dō in Hyōgo Prefecture, and the great southern gate of Tōdai-ji, the Nandaimon, are built in this style.

The Castle

From the latter half of the Medieval Period the needs of war diverted the energies of the nation from the building of temples to the building of castles. The castle had its origins in the forts of the ancient period in the northeastern districts of Japan. Remains of these forts show that troops were provided with quarters in a defensive stronghold.

In the medieval wars strongholds were established on the top of a hill with temporary dwelling quarters for the warriors at the base. The stronghold developed into a fort surrounded by heavy earthen ramparts and log fences. These were defences against warriors on horseback, and the selection of the site was most important. Generally sites were steep hills rising suddenly from a valley, or a hill rising suddenly from a river bed, with an artificial cliff built out onto the slope behind the fort, as at Minowa Castle whose remains exist near Takasaki. The interior of the fort was divided into several strongholds: if one fell, the defenders could retreat to the next stronghold and continue the fighting.

In the middle of the sixteenth century the gun was introduced into Japan, possibly from a Portuguese ship wrecked off the coast of Tanegashima, an island in southern Kyūshū, or possibly from China. Guns were used shortly thereafter in battles in the central district of Japan, and their use spread quickly. This necessitated changes in the construction of the forts, which were now encircled with a strong rampart of stonework surmounted by a heavy earthen wall. This wall was sometimes combined with a 'yagura', or storehouse.

In the eighth century the 'yagura' was an arms stack for bows and arrows, but by the tenth century the word meant an observatory. In the painted scrolls of the medieval period the 'yagura' is shown as a high platform above the entrance gate, walled with shields to provide protection while shooting at the enemy.

In 1558, a castle in central Japan had a two storied 'yagura', the upper floor being both an observatory and a shrine for the war god. This is a prototype of the main keep, the 'tenshukaku' of later castles. In 1566, Oda Nobunaga established a castle with walls 2,000 ken, about 4,000 yards in circumference, surmounted by ten houses and ten observatories. This was the origin of the idea of recent castles. In the same period a castle near Nara included a house called 'Tamon-yagura' in the encircling wall.

In 1576, Nobunaga constructed Azuchi Castle on the eastern shore of Lake Biwa with a commanding view of the side plain, marking the beginning of the second period of castle construction. The warriors' quarters were now at the foot of the castle. Three years after the walls were completed, a central seven-storied keep was constructed atop the 65-foot high battlement. Nobunaga's high keep in Azuchi Castle set a fashion, for in the year 1558 alone, twenty-five 'tenshukaku' were built. Occasionally they comprised a complex of small and large keeps, as in the Himeji Castle. They were constructed not only as observatories and living quarters, but as the symbol of the war lord's authority over the battlefield and the surrounding districts. As Nobunaga's authority increased in the land, so the long period of wars tended to end. The castles proved also to be the impetus for urban growth, as artisans, craftsmen, and merchants settled around them to form the nuclei of the 'jōka machi'–castle towns–which were to be the centres of culture for three centuries thereafter.

With the introduction of guns, castle sites were changed to meet the challenge, leaving the mountains in favor of small hills separated by deep ditches and moats from the open plains. The plan of this enclosure was a labyrinth of spaces with concealed entrances spiralling up to the highest story of the central keep, in which invaders might go astray and be repulsed from the next stronghold. The fundamental idea of castle construction at this time was to strengthen the castle itself, its site, and also the country of the war lord, against attack. This involved planning on a regional scale, and whole towns were designed for defensive reasons, as in early Edo (Tōkyō), where the town was enclosed by an earthen rampart or moat.

The essential part of Himeji Castle belongs to this second stage of castle construction; it was enlarged in 1617 to its present size. Two years before the last enlargement of Himeji Castle, Tokugawa Ieyasu, the founder of the Edo 'bakufu', under which Japan remained at peace for the next three centuries, ordered the destruction of all castles, except for one in each district, which was to be maintained as the seat of the local government. Of a few thousand castles and forts only about two hundred remained. In Harima, a part of the present Hyōgo Prefecture, one-hundred forty-seven forts and thirty-eight strongholds were completely destroyed. The lords of the remaining castles required licenses from the central government at Edo to carry out repairs or alterations. This edict ended Japan's age of castle building.

The Dwelling

One of the relics excavated from the sepulchral mounds of the fourth century in Samida, Nara Prefecture, is a Japanese bronze mirror with a relief

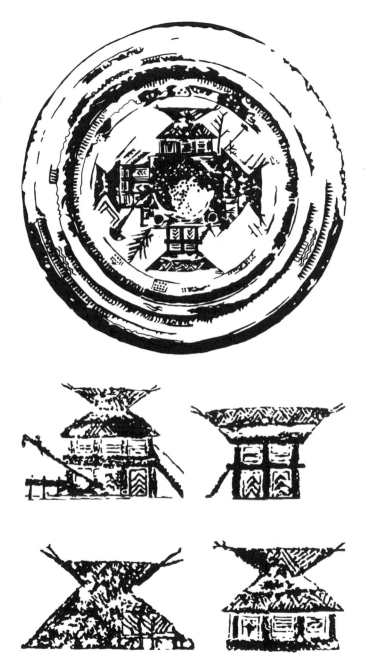

Back of a mirror, representing four buildings (4th c.)

93

pattern of four houses on its back. These houses are believed to represent the residential style of the chieftans of the period, and may even depict the domicile of the man who was buried in that mound. One, which has a high floor, is generally thought to have been a warehouse. However, drawings of houses on both bronze bells and pottery of the Yayoi Period have a similar post and beam construction and gabled roof, but none of the warehouses excavated to date use post and beam construction. They all have load-bearing walls of thick wooden boards. We therefore cannot be certain whether the first house on the mirror is a warehouse or a dwelling.

The next house also has a high floor and is regarded as a dwelling because of its relatively larger scale. In both these houses the space beneath the floor appears to be enclosed by something, but its purpose is not clear. This second house has a veranda, and a hanging sunshade called 'kinugasa'.

Another house shows only a large roof, and obviously represents a pit dwelling, with its floor below ground level. The house also has the combination of veranda and sunshade attached to one side of the hanging entrance door, indicating that the pit dwellers spent some time sitting in the shade. It may be this 'kinugasa' which later developed into the uniquely Japanese covered open space called 'hisashi'. Thus the germ of the feeling for open space in later Japanese houses is apparent in everyday life as early as the fourth century.

The last house is the most formal, and although it has a thatched roof, it is built on an earthen platform. It resembles a Buddha Hall, but as Buddhism had hardly taken root in China in the fourth century, the exact function of this building is unknown. It was probably a nonutilitarian building, and was not a native structure; it was imported, in both form and function, from the continent. We may assume that these four houses show us the main forms of Japanese architecture in the fourth century.

There are a few extant records of the houses of Nara in the eighth century, when it was the capital of Japan. They show a house with a wooden board floor and a thatched roof of cypress bark, earthen floored houses with thatched or board roofs, and warehouses with load bearing walls of horizontally laid logs. This warehouse construction is common in northern Asia, and is called 'azekura zukuri'.

In 724, the government issued orders encouraging buildings in the continental style, with tile roofs and painted columns and beams, and probably all of the government offices were constructed in this way, but the Imperial Palace was built in the native Japanese tradition with cypress bark thatch and wooden floors. It is possible to visualize the Imperial Palace of this period from a restoration of the house of the Tachibana family, which was rebuilt and dedicated to Hōryū-ji Temple, although its exterior style has since been changed.

There is also a detailed record of one minister's house which gives us an excellent idea of the aristocratic residence of the eighth century, although this record differs from the Tachibana house. It has timber floor boards and a board roof. Both houses have a covered open space with a veranda, but in the Tachibana house this open space, which comprises 40% of the area, seems to be copied from the traditional continental palace. The minister's house consists of a central section, called the 'moya', with thick circular columns, and on two sides of the 'moya' is an open space, the 'hisashi', which is covered by a lean-to board roof and supported by thin square pillars. The 'hisashi' had played an important role in the evolution of the dwelling in ancient times; it was added gradually to the four sides of the 'moya' and finally completely enclosed it. Then surrounding these 'hisashi' was a second space of similar construction called 'mago-hisashi'. This formal arrangement of 'moya' and 'hisashi' is a typical spatial organization of the interior of 'shinden zukuri'.

The 'Shinden zukuri' Style

Surrounding the main hall, the 'Shinden', were secondary independent buildings the 'tainoya', to the east, west and north, which also follow the same principle of interior space organization as the 'Shinden'. To the south is an artificial lake with an island in the centre, and facing the lake on either side of the main hall is a pavilion, or 'Izumi-dono', the fountain pavilion. Utilitarian buildings—the kitchens and servants quarters—were located at the back and sides of the main group of buildings, and the whole complex was connected by galleries and corridors, some of which had roofs.

The use of the 'shinden zukuri' for the integration of the whole, as well as for all the independent buildings, is typical of the aristocratic residential style of the Heian Era. The interior of these residences thus consisted of a series of isolated spaces, connected by covered or open galleries which not only gave continuity to the whole plan, but articulated the parts of the exterior garden courts as well. The gardens were connected with each other visually, as the galleries had open sides. These concepts of the isolation and the connection of spaces at the same time have been basic to development of the spatial organization in Japan.

The 'Shoin zukuri' Style

The Middle Ages were a time of violent disturbances. The elegant ceremonies of the aristocrats of the Heian Court, which often were held in the 'Shinden' of aristocratic residences, were displaced by practical matters of living and disrupted by the fighting between powerful territorial magnates. At first this residence became the model for the war-lords and their warriors, but in the process of adaptation, the traditional aristocratic residence underwent several changes. The main hall, which before had simply been partitioned by folding screens, was now divided into several chambers by sliding doors, and the thick circular columns of the 'moya' were replaced by thin square pillars, as in the 'hisashi', which was more economical, and fitted better with the sliding doors. The wooden floors were now covered with 'tatami', tightly woven thin grass mats covering straw mats about two inches thick, and the heavy top-hung wooden doors, which had comprised the external partitions in the ancient houses, were changed to light-weight wooden sliding doors or wood-frame and paper sliding doors, called 'shōji'. In the main chamber a 'tokonoma', or alcove, 'tana' shelves of different heights, and a window with a fixed desk called

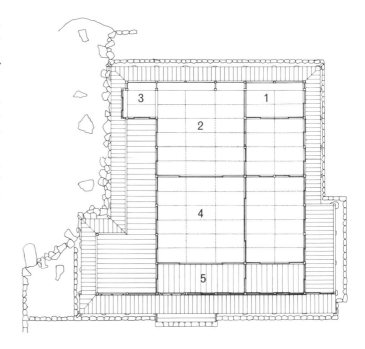

Plan of the Kōjoin at Miidera, near Ōtsu

1 cloakroom (nando)
2 main room (kamiza)
3 raised portion (jōdan)
4 'the next room' (tsugi-no-ma)
5 entrance for receptions (kuge-no-ma)

'shoin-mado' were built in as one unit. This chamber became known as the 'shoin' and the whole style as the 'shoin zukuri'. It reached its highest expression in the residences of the feudal lords in the early seventeenth century.

A typical lord's residence consisted of a vestibule and guard room, or 'tōzamurai', a large official room, the 'hiroma', a meeting room, the 'taimen-sho', and a study, the 'shoin'. The 'taiman-sho' was used both for private and official meetings, and the 'shoin' was for private use. There was also a stage for 'Nō'-dramas in front of the main building, and a separate pavilion for tea ceremonies located elsewhere. The women's quarters, 'goten', or maids' quarters, the 'tsubone', and the warehouses and kitchens, were behind the main buildings.

The structure, plan form, and decoration of the main buildings were repeated in the 'goten' and 'tsubone'. There was a lavish atmosphere inside the rooms, as the sliding doors, walls and ceilings were painted in rich colours. This art form could only be fully appreciated when all the doors were closed.

The 'taimen-sho' of Nijō Castle and Nishi-Honganji are the best extant examples of the 'shoin zukuri' style.

Although the formation of the 'shoin' was a direct historical development of the 'shinden zukuri', by the time the style finally evolved the heavy central 'moya' had disappeared, and the interior space became a combination of all the open 'hisashi'. The various apartments, unlike the extended formal plan of the 'shinden zukuri', were assembled and arranged more organically, according to their function, and connected where necessary by closed corridors. Although the interiors were divided with sliding doors, these could be removed, and the interior of the 'shoin zukuri' then resembled that of the 'shinden zukuri'.

The gardens of the lords' residences in the beginning of the Middle Ages were in the Heian Period 'shinden zukuri' style, but later, in the Muromachi Period, a new type evolved which combined this style with that of the newly established Zen garden style.

The 'Sukiya zukuri' Style

Parallel with the development of the 'shoin zukuri' was the development of the 'sukiya zukuri', or a pavilion style. The idea of a pavilion for various kinds of entertainment – especially the tea ceremony – located in a garden was introduced from the continent, and developed side by side with 'shoin zukuri'. The two forms – 'sukiya zukuri' and 'shoin zukuri' had developmental influence upon each other. 'Sukiya zukuri' had no strict, pragmatic necessities, no formal canons, and its main characteristic was one of extreme freedom through flexibility. Some of the finest examples are the Katsura and Shugakuin detached palaces, and the Sankei-en, in Yokohama,

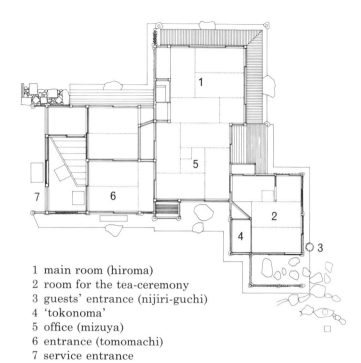

1 main room (hiroma)
2 room for the tea-ceremony
3 guests' entrance (nijiri-guchi)
4 'tokonoma'
5 office (mizuya)
6 entrance (tomomachi)
7 service entrance

Plan of the Ryōkaku-tei, the tea-pavilion of the Ninna-ji Temple, Kyōto

the villa of a feudal lord.

In 'shoin zukuri' the war lords had discarded the elegant rituals of the imperial court, and modified the formal 'shinden zukuri' style. Their ceremonies and houses, with the hierarchical arrangement of the various private and public rooms, mirrored the power structure of society. The earlier 'sukiya zukuri' and tea houses were built primarily by decadent aristocrats, scholarly priests and the newly risen wealthy merchant class, who all stood outside the samurai power hierarchy. The airy atmosphere and the free spatiality of the 'sukiya zukuri' echoes this freedom from the exercise of power. The tea house – chashitsu' – evolved from the same principles as the 'sakiya zukuri', but the extremely small, fully enclosed interior, and the garden, attained a unique degree of metaphysical expression – especially in the 'chashitsu' designed by Sen no Rikyū, and his grandson, Sōtan – far beyond the older style.

Plates

Nijō Castle
(Kyōto)

101 In the foreground is the Ni-no-maru, or central stronghold, with the Hon-maru, the main stronghold, to the rear. There was a Tenshu, or central keep, within the Hon-maru, which was lost in a fire, and never reconstructed. In the foreground of the Ni-no-maru is the Tō-zamurai, or waiting hall, and behind it, the Shikidai, or meeting hall, and the Ō-hiroma, or reception rooms. To the rear are the Kuro-shoin and the Shiro-shoin, the private drawing rooms and residence of the 'shōgun'.

102 Gable detail of the Tō-zamurai.

103 The façade of the Ō-hiroma.

Nishi-Hongan-ji
(Kyōto)

104 Kuro-shoin, the private rooms of the chief priest.

105 Another view of the same room. To the right the corner of the Tokonoma, and to the left the library (tana). The abbots of the Zen monastery disposed their books on shelves distributed in the walls of their room; from this custom came the 'tana' of the residences of the Shoin style, with the asymetric shelves in precious woods, maintained with gilted bronze fittings, finely engraved.

106 The interior of the Taimensho, the reception hall, showing the general atmosphere of the Shoin-zukuri style of residence.

107 Shiro-shoin, the private drawing rooms.

108 The transom of the Kuro-shoin.

109 Kuro-shoin. The covered open space, showing the basin and stepping stones.

Kōjo-in, Mii-dera, Ōtsu
(Shiga Prefecture)

110 The Hor-in, or veranda, of the guest hall, built in 1601 seen from the garden.

Kangaku-in, Mii-dera, Ōtsu
(Shiga Prefecture)

111 Hio-en, the covered open space. Built two years after the Kōjo-in.

Himeji Castle
(Hyōgō Prefecture)

112 The complex of the central stronghold. The central main keep is combined with three smaller keeps. Under reconstruction.

113 The inner moat and the main keeps.

114 The path to the main keeps.

115 Looking down from the main keep, over a smaller keep, to the first entrance gate, which incorporates its own keep.

116 The Tenshu, or main keep.

Nijo Castle, Ninomaru densha
General plan 1:4000, elevations 1:300

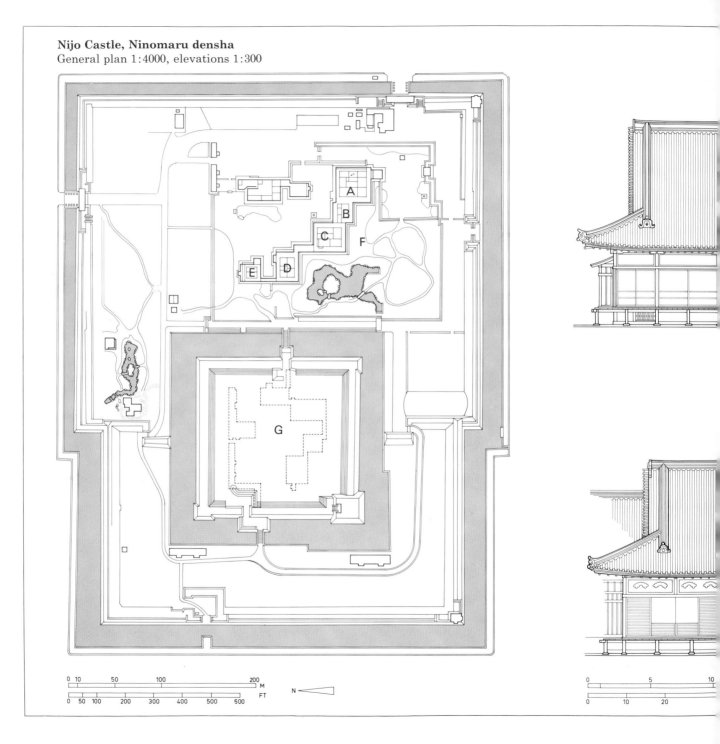

0 10   50   100   200
                        M
0 50 100 200 300 400 500 600
                        FT

N

0   5   10

0   10   20

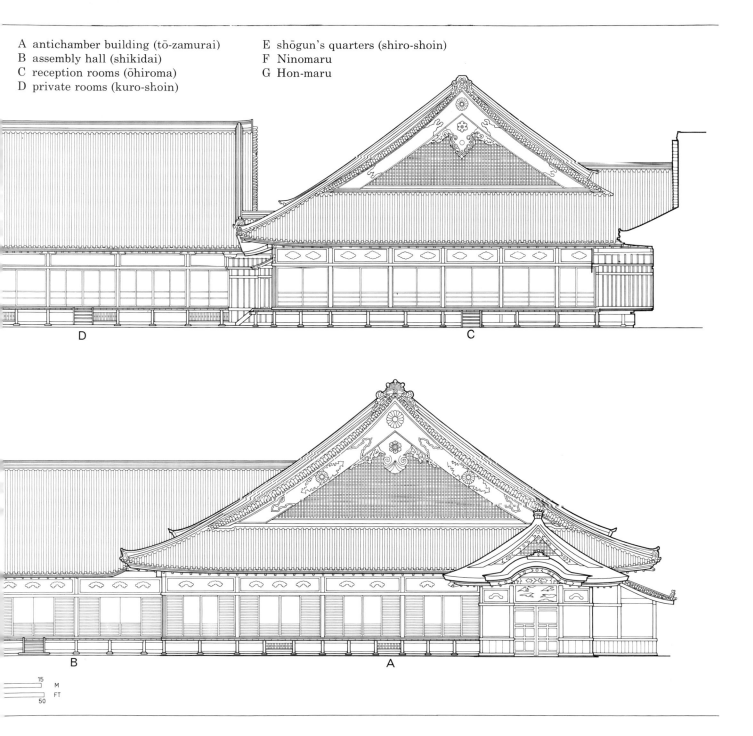

A antichamber building (tō-zamurai)
B assembly hall (shikidai)
C reception rooms (ōhiroma)
D private rooms (kuro-shoin)

E shōgun's quarters (shiro-shoin)
F Ninomaru
G Hon-maru

D

C

B

A

15
M

50
FT

Notes

The Use of the Carpenter's Square

In ancient times the slope of the end of a hipped roof was sometimes made different from that of the main roof for visual reasons, and the joining of the kioi, the rail on the end of the first rafters, and the haitsuke taruki, the short rafters at the corners, to the hip rafter, called in this case furisumigi, became very complicated. The joints were made very loosely, by a process of trial and error, at the actual joining site. Although there was not sufficient technical knowledge to make proper structural joints, the carpenters' main concern was to develop the form as a whole as an object of aesthetic appreciation. During the middle ages however, the technology for the precise finishing of the eaves details was perfected. The carpenter's square was rapidly developed, and the use of the urame scale was probably perfected between the 13th and 14th centuries, making it possible to cut complicated joints on the ground (see below).

The kane shaku, or carpenter's square which has been popular from around the 14th century, is an 'L' shaped steel scale, graduated on both sides. One side is graduated in a scale called omote or omoteme. The long arm is 1 shaku and 5–6 sun long, and the short arm is 7.5–8 sun long, divided such that 1 shaku = 10 sun, 1 sun = 10 bu, 1 bu = 10 rin, where 1 shaku = 11.9″. On the other side the short arm is also graduated with the omote scale, but the long arm is graduated into shaku and sun with a scale called urame or uragane such that 1 shaku urame = $\sqrt{2}$ shaku omote.

For skilful use of the square, various kinds of inclinations had to be studied and measured beforehand.

Assume a right angle triangle ABC where the base AB = 1 shaku. Then the length BC measures the inclination of the hypotenuse AC to the base AB since the gradient of AC = $\frac{CB}{AB}$ = $\frac{CB}{1}$ = CB.

That is, to measure the inclination of a member two lines are drawn directly on the member at right angles, one horizontal, yokomizu, and the other vertical, tatemizu, or mizu. Using the omote scale the long arm is placed on the horizontal line such that the length = 1 shaku, then the inclination of the member can be read on the short arm omote scale on the vertical line. This measurement of inclination in terms of length is one of the basic uses of the car-

penter's square. The inclination of 1 shaku means an inclination of 45°, and is called kane kōbai. An inclination to the horizontal is called kōbai, e. g. the gradient of the rafters, and an inclination to the vertical is called nage kōbai, as in the slope of the outer surface of kioi, the rail at the end of rafters. It was necessary to know these inclinations in order to construct the joints, and they were measured directly from the square.

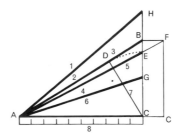 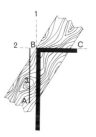

1 = chōgen-kōbai	5 = nobikane-kōbai
2 = chōgen	6 = tangen-kōbai
3 = tangen	7 = chūkō
4 = chūkō-kōbai	8 = 1 shaku

1 = tatemizu
2 = yokomizu
3 = 1 shaku

Let ABC be any right triangle whose base AC = 1 shaku. By constructing the perpendicular from C to the hypotenuse, we obtain the line CD, known as the chūkō. Swing an arc from C of radius CD, to intersect BC at the point E. The inclination of the line AE, as measured by the distance CE, is called the chūkō-kōbai. Extend AC to a point C′ such that AC′ = AB, and drop a perpendicular from a point F to AC′ at C′, such that C′F = BC, and draw the line AF. It will be seen that for any right triangle, the point E must fall on AF. Thus the inclination of AF, the nobikane-kōbai, is equal to the inclination of AE, the chūkō-kōbai. Extend BC to a point H, such that CH = AD. The inclination of AH, as measured by CH, is known as the chōgen-kōbai. DB is known as the tangen; find the point G on BC such that DB = CG. The inclination of AG, measured by BG, is called tangen-kōbai.

(Continuation p. 138.)

100

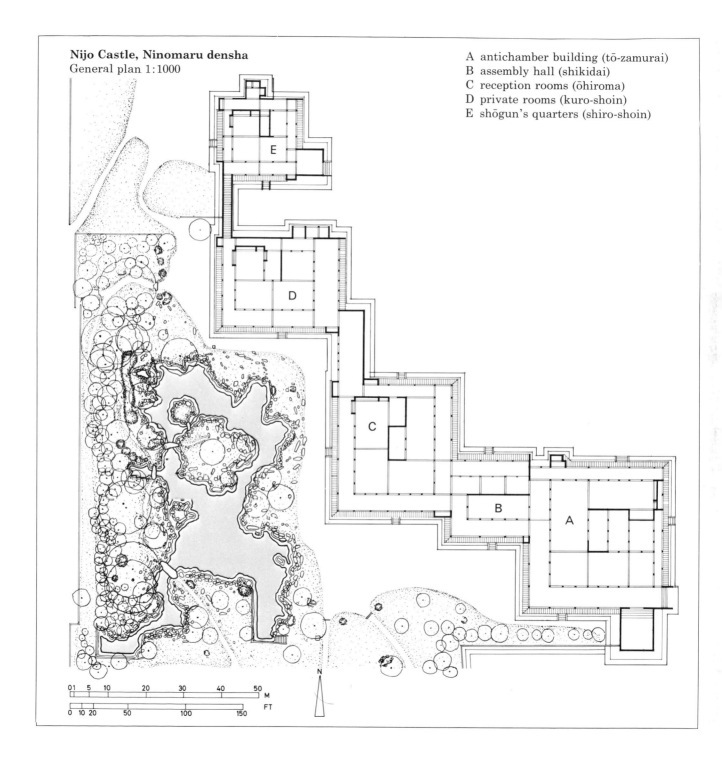

Nijo Castle, Ninomaru densha
General plan 1:1000

A antichamber building (tō-zamurai)
B assembly hall (shikidai)
C reception rooms (ōhiroma)
D private rooms (kuro-shoin)
E shōgun's quarters (shiro-shoin)

E

D

C

B

A

N

01 5 10   20   30   40   50
M

0 10 20   50   100   150
FT

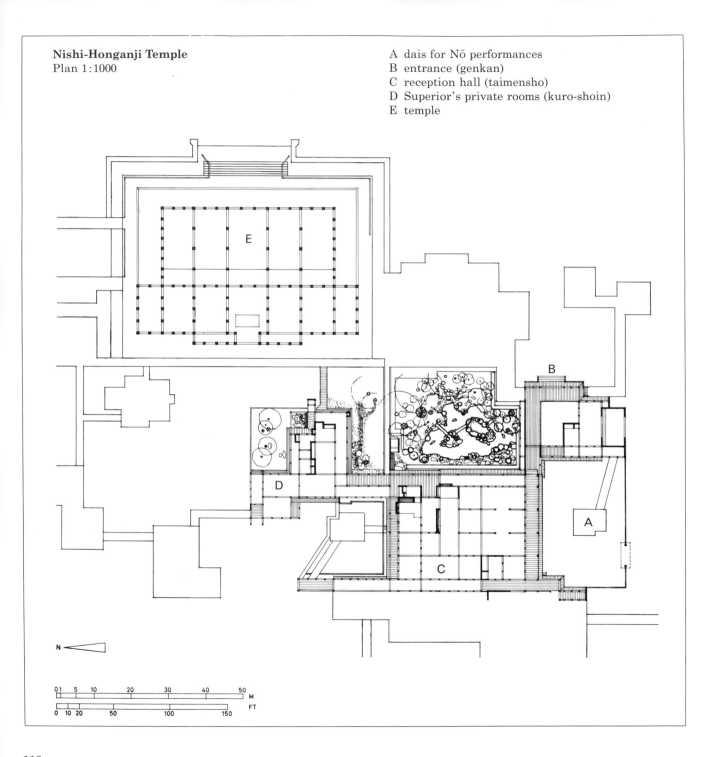

Nishi-Honganji Temple
Plan 1:1000

A dais for Nō performances
B entrance (genkan)
C reception hall (taimensho)
D Superior's private rooms (kuro-shoin)
E temple

N

0 1 5 10   20   30   40   50
                                             M
0 10 20   50   100   150
                                        FT

3. Structure and Techniques

Materials

Nearly all building materials were of vegetable origin. Because of the temperate, humid climate, over 90% of the ancient Japanese islands were covered with forests. Despite the policies of forest conservation practised by the Tokugawa 'Bakufu', however, due to field cultivation and indiscriminate felling for building purposes, the forest coverage had decreased to 80% by the beginning of this century. Now it is around 60%.

The principal timber species used were the conifers such as cedar, pine, cypress and fir, for structural materials, and such deciduous trees as oak and chestnut for furniture and fixtures. Paper made from the mulberry tree was used for the sliding paper 'shōji', and bamboo was used for the wall lathing which was coated with a mixture of clay, sand and straw fibres, or with a variety of hydrated lime made of limestone or oyster shells. The 'tatami' mat, the principal floor covering, was made of beaten rice straw covered with a tightly woven mat of rush.

Except for the ramparts of the castles, stone was used in architecture only as the base for posts and pillars. Clay, however, was used extensively, not only for the entire wall, from its core to its final coating, but also for producing roof tiles. Before the seventeenth century, a tile called 'hongawara' was used, similar to the Spanish Mission Barrel variety, but since that time a new type of tile called 'sangawara' has been employed, especially in civilian town houses. This tile was of comparatively light weight and of a lapped-edge construction.

Japanese structures therefore were almost invariably built of wood, despite the frequent serious damage caused by fires, typhoons and earthquakes. This fatalism which considered the house as temporary and transient, had prevailed since the Middle Ages.

Carpenter Organization

Under the ancient 'Ritsuryō-sei' system, official architecture was under the direction of a bureau called Mokuryo, which was part of the 'Kūnai shō', or Imperial Household Ministry. Special temporary offices existed to supervise constructions, such as the 'Zōkyō-shi', office for the construction of the capital, the 'Zōkyū-shi', office for the construction of the Imperial palace, and 'Zōji-shi', for the building of important shrines and temples. These temporary offices were not included in the legal organization of the government, but existed only for the benefit of the Imperial Household.

The artisans who belonged both to the legal institutions, the 'Mokuryō', and the temporary offices, were mainly naturalized Japanese or their descendants whose skills were passed down from their forebears in China and Korea.

In the Heian Period, apart from the 'Mokuryō', there was a bureau, the 'Suri-shiki', for the maintenance of government buildings. This was a large official guild of artisans which included master carpenters – called 'daikō' – and common carpenters – called 'shōkō'. As 'shōen', private manors, were gradually established by the influential temples, shrines and powerful aristocratic families, owing largely to the decline of the ancient 'Ritsuryō' legal system, these carpenters joined the offices of the 'Zōji-shō', which constructed new temples, and 'Suri-shō' which maintained existing temples. Both of these offices were attached to such important temples as Tōdai-ji and Tōji.

The carpenters of Hida Privince, known as 'Hida-no-takumi', were considered the foremost craftsmen of their day. They were often exempted from all taxes and corvées, and instead called to work on the official buildings of the capital. Because they spent alternate years in the provinces, and then in the capital, they were also known as 'bansho'. Later, they became employees of the aristocracy, the shrines, and the temples, and some of them eventually settled in 'shōen' villages and were attached to powerful families, who paid them a rice salary. Others were travelling carpenters, who found work on the large construction projects in the provinces, where there was much new building activity after the end of the Neian Period.

About the twelfth century there were non-official temporary organizations of carpenters engaged in private construction initiated by the powerful local magnates. The carpenters in these organizations were divided into the various categories of 'daikō', the chief carpenter in charge of all construction works, 'indo', master carpenter, 'otona', qualified carpenters, and 'tsura', common carpenters. A typical organization of a building site recorded in the twelfth century consisted of one 'daikō', two 'indo' and eight 'tsura'. Another had one 'daikō', two 'indo', twelve 'otona' and fifty-eight 'tsura'.

In the twelfth century, 'za', a system of merchants' guilds and many kinds of artisans' guilds was formed. A guild usually belonged to an influential temple or shrine and had certain privileges. The 'za' of carpenters were free to contract for the construction of any kind of building in any location, and were no longer subject to government control. The 'Nara-daiku', traditional Nara carpenters, and 'Kyō-daiku', carpenters trained in Kyoto, became quite famous. Until the latter half of the thirteenth century these 'za' were granted exclusive rights to construct and maintain the temples and shrines to which they belonged. In return for these privileges the members of the 'za' paid a tax to the temples, the 'daiku bunin ryō', or some labour service. Sometimes these privileges did not belong to a 'za', but to an influential carpenter family. The exclusive right held by a family to work for a temple or shrine was called 'daiku shiki', and was inherited by the son or could be sold.

About the fifteenth century this custom was replaced by contract work, where the chief carpenter was called 'daiku', and his name inscribed on a wooden board, or 'munafuda', which was hung under the ridgepole.

In the Medieval Period small groups of carpenters were formed under an apprenticeship system, and the distinction made between 'miya-daiku', shrine carpenters, and 'tera-daiku', temple carpenters, disappeared. Some of these 'nakama', or groups, had over twenty apprentices, and the carpenters became known as 'machi-daiku', or civil carpenters. Often these carpenters belonged to the warlords, engaged in building castles or in military service, and were paid a rice stipend, as were the 'samurai'. These carpenters were drawn from the upper echelons of the famous carpenter families. Other carpenters worked on the construction of castles and castle towns, which were the main construction activities of the sixteenth and seventeenth centuries.

With the establishment of the Tokugawa 'Bakufu' in the seventeenth century, and the prohibition of the construction of castles, the employment by feudal lords of those other than famous carpenters decreased, and carpenters became free artisans who lived in the castle towns, without privileges. The names of the master carpenters, 'daiku', 'tōryō' and 'bansho' came to be general professional names.

The construction sites, the carpenters, and their methods, were illustrated in picture scrolls after the twelfth century. The instruments illustrated included the 'ken sao' and the 'shaku zue', long measures made by the carpenters and used for ground surveys and for measuring long timbers, the 'kane shaku', a carpenter's square (see below), the 'sumitsubo', for drawing directly on the timber, and 'mizuito' and 'suijunki' for checking levelness. The tools used were the 'masakari', the big axe, the 'chōna', a

Carpenters' tools

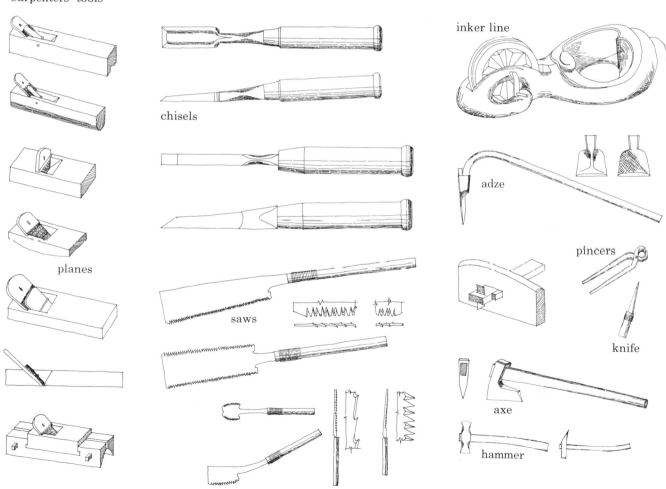

chisels

planes

saws

inker line

adze

pincers

knife

axe

hammer

type of adze, the 'yoki', an axe for chopping, the 'nokogiri', a saw, the 'kiri', a gimlet, the 'nomi', a chisel, the 'yariganna', a plane, the 'saizuchi', a wooden mallet, the 'tsuchi', a hammer, etc., all of which had been used from ancient times, and many of which are still commonly used today.

In the Muromachi Period (1336–1573), the 'ōga', a big saw, was imported from Ming China, and took the place of the ancient method of splitting wood with an axe. The sawyers became one of the most important professional groups.

About A.D. 1600 the 'dai-kanna', a handplane, was invented, making possible a rapid increase in the production of wooden boards, and also improving surface finishing techniques. Thereafter, various types of hand planes, saws, chisels and gimlets were introduced, greatly enhancing the development of various types of joints.

Among the medieval picture scrolls there is a scene of the work of a 'miya-daiku', a shrine carpenter, which shows a man-high working drawing of the side elevation of a 'nagare zukuri' style shrine. At that time the master carpenters probably made such drawings, but later these were made by specialists called 'ezu-shi'. The master carpenters also made drawings directly on the timber, called 'sumitsuke', which became increasingly complicated with the development of regular and precise finishing details. These drawings were possible only with the skillful use of the 'kane-shaku', the carpenter's square.

The Structural System

The structural solution to the problem of covering large spaces in the ancient palaces and temples was a post and beam construction, imported from China. Long beams, supported by two inner posts, spanned the central space, with smaller beams, joining the

Kondō of the Tōshōdai-ji Temple, Nara: transverse section

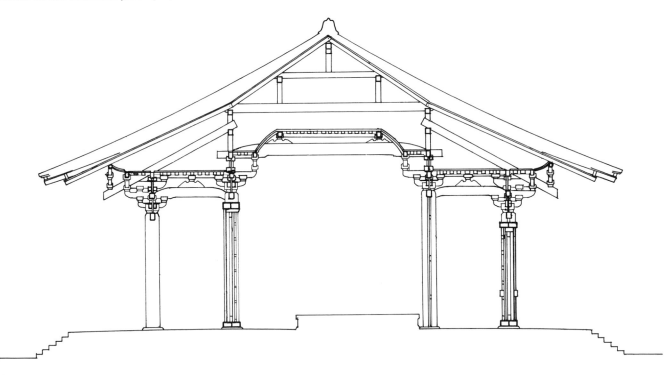

inner and outer posts, spanning the peripheral spaces. This resulted in a large central space, either with narrower spaces along two sides, or completely surrounded by a narrower space. This structural system was not rigid in three dimensions, as only the purlins connected the structure in the longitudinal direction. This merely two dimensional solution was probably structurally sufficient for the Chinese mainland where there were no earthquakes.

When the temples simply housed an image of Buddha, this symmetrical cross section and plan was ideal, but some time later in the building of temples there was a need for a ritual space in front of the image. In Japan, this was at first provided by making the cross-section asymmetrical, as in the 'Kondo', or central hall of Tōshōdaiji, 759. The structural system followed the Chinese tradition, and the area under the small span at the front of the building was opened to the outside for worshippers. The image was placed to the rear of the central space, and the area in front of the image was used as a ritual space.

Another solution for the accommodation of worshippers was that of 'Hokke-dō' of Tōdai-ji. This was an independent hall close to the front of the Buddha Hall, constructed in the same manner. The building existing today is the result of changes in the Kamakura Period.

In the 'Konpon-chūdō', the central hall of Enryaku ji, a worshippers' hall, or 'Raidō', was added in A.D. 980 at the front of the building, and covered by extending the roof of the 'Konpon-chūdō' downward on one side. The present plan of this hall was then established. This was probably at first a lean-to roof of the 'hisashi' type which was very popular at the time, especially for extending interior spaces. Later, when this building was destroyed by fire in 1435, the extension was integrated with the main roof and a large, symmetrical hipped-gable roof was built, made possible by the new structural techniques of the Middle Ages.

The plan and structure of the Buddha Hall also developed in the Middle Ages because of this same need to provide a worshipping space in front of the image. There were three logical ways to solve this problem: first, to move the Buddha altar backward;

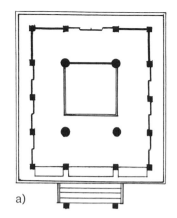

a)

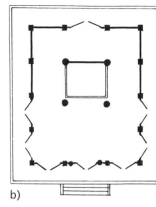

b)

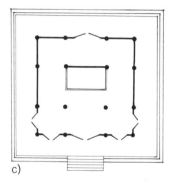

c)

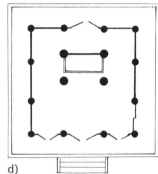

d)

a) Hondō of the Sanzen-in, near Kyōto (about 1148)
b) Hondō of the Fuki-dera, Oita (about the 12th c.)
c) Amida-dō (Shiramizu) of the Ganjō-ji Temple, Fukushima (1160)
d) Amida-dō of the Myodo-ji Temple, Kumamoto (about 1229)
e) Omidō of the Chishiki-dera Temple, Nagano (about the 16th c.)

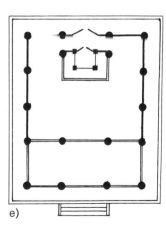

e)

Plans showing the evolution of structural systems

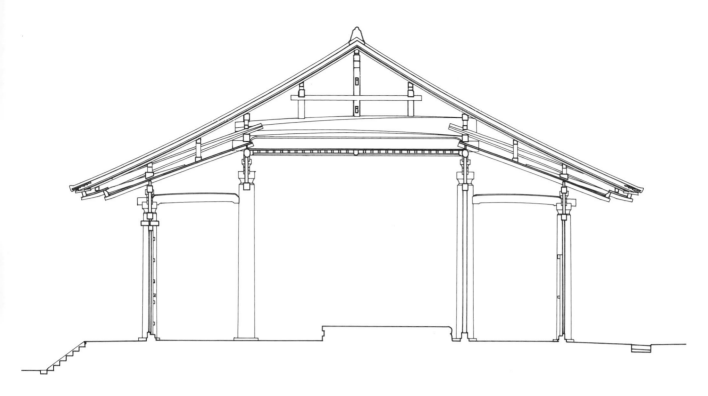

Kōdō of the Horyū-ji Temple, Nara: transverse section
(after Professor Asano)

second, to extend the depth of the forward part of the building; and third, a combination of both these methods.

All these methods were attempted in the Middle Ages. The pillars of the inner temple, the 'shitenbashira', were moved further back, or two of the frontal inner pillars were removed, to leave only the rear pillars, the 'raigo-bashira', at the same time decreasing the depth of the altar. This was characteristic especially of small Buddhist Halls of the Middle Ages such as the 'Sangendō', the Hall of Three Bays, and the 'Gokendō', the Hall of Five Bays. The front part of the hall could be extended either by widening the outer span at the front, or by adding an extra span. This latter solution was the principal method of spatial organization of medieval Buddhist halls.

The Ceiling

The ceiling evolved separately from the rest of the structure and covered the whole plan, even under the eaves. By changing the height or the form of the ceiling over the various interior parts, each spatial function was symbolically defined, without relation to the divisions by the posts of the structure. The ceilings of tea houses were used in this way in a later period.

After the end of the tenth century a kind of ceiling was built under the eaves which had a similar appearance to the real eave structure; the latter was called 'no yane', ground roof, and the former, 'keshō yane', the finishing or decorative roof. The earliest example is the 'Kōdō' at Horyuji. The 'keshō yane' eliminated the traditional problems posed by deep projecting eaves with bracket-supported rafters, and the problem of spacing the rafters and brackets for a pleasing visual effect, as it was now completely hidden between the roof and the ceiling. It developed into a uniquely Japanese structural system. The technique of building the 'keshō yane' combined with the block and bracket system, 'masu gumi', gave the appearance of a real and precise structure. This inconsistency between the real structure and the implied structure, this softening of the interior vertical dimension, allowed a visual expression of precision and delicacy and a gentle, human feeling for space. These were to become characteristics of Japanese architecture.

The Roof Structure

Since ancient times the shape of the roof had been an aesthetic consideration. In the ancient temples there was little discrepance between the plan and the section, but as the plan changed to accommodate the worshippers, the traditional symmetry of the cross-section was destroyed. In order to construct a symmetrical roof and to have the freedom to choose its slope, but still to be able to plan without the restrictions of regular column spacing, two new structural innovations were developed.

The first, 'Shariden-eden', 1219, at Hōryūji Temple, was achieved by the skillful use of double beams, despite the use of the traditional two dimensional construction. The lower register of beams spanned between the columns as usual, with the columns spaced according to the plan requirements, and not necessarily cross-sectionally symmetrical about the central axis. The upper beams were then supported on short posts resting on the lower beam, without regard to the position of the columns, thus solving the problem of a symmetrical roof over an asymmetric plan.

The second development was that of a three dimensional roof structure, which enabled the free choice of the roof slope. In ancient temples the post and beam structure was not rigid, as the joints were loosely constructed. The only connections between the columns were beams called 'kashira nuki', notched through the tops of the columns by alternately working the end of the beam and the end of the column until they fitted. This trial and error method was also used in the construction of the block and bracket system supporting the wide overhang of the eaves, resulting in each bracket being a different size as in the Hōō-dō of the Byōdō-in, 1053. In the 'Kannon-dō' of the Byōdō-in, at an earlier period in the Middle Ages, the ends of the ridgepole, which did not necessarily correspond with the columns or beams of the main structure in the hipped roof construction, were supported by two posts which stood on two lengthwise end-beams at each end of the building. In other, later edifices, a single beam was employed, running the entire length of the building, with vertical supports for the ridgepole placed at intervals unrelated to the columns below; in earlier structures, two end-beams had been used. This single beam was known as the 'jimune'.

The development of a three dimensional structure began with the reinforcement of the columns. The horizontal members, 'koshinuki', connecting the columns below floor level, first appeared in the main hall of Daihoon-ji, 1227, in Kyoto. Other horizontal members, called 'hinuki', joined the upper parts of the columns in the main hall of Gokuraku-dō, 1244, in Nara, while the posts which supported the purlins in this building were also joined by thin rails. This connection of the columns horizontally with thin rails lengthwise and crosswise was a refinement used later in the early seventeenth century.

About a century later, in 1359, we find in the main hall of Ishizu-dera, in Shiga Prefecture, beams spanned between the columns in both directions; this use of lengthwise beams was the first major break with traditional structure. In this temple the symmetrical cross-section had completely disappeared, and longitudinally there were two displaced posts in the rear row of the central space. The purlins were supported by posts at regular intervals having no relationship to the column spacing. These posts, which were connected by thin rails, were supported on three large girders running the length of the building, and on the beams which spanned in both directions between the columns. These girders were supported on two-cross beams which spanned from the two irregular columns, over the lengthwise beams, and were supported on short posts. These posts rested on the tie beams at the front of the hall.

This structural system was quite different from the Chinese prototype, and in combination with flat ceil-ings which concealed the roof structure, made free organization of interior space possible, and allowed the slope of the roof to be chosen to suit aesthetic requirements.

In the early thirteenth century a cantilever, called 'hanegi', was invented, supporting the real eaves structure as described. The apparent eave under the real one was suspended from the 'hanegi', which made the construction of this implied structure easier. In the fifteenth century 'gagyō hanegi' was invented. This was a cantilever which supported the detached

Plan of the main building of the Daihoon-ji Temple, Kyōto: floor and ceiling

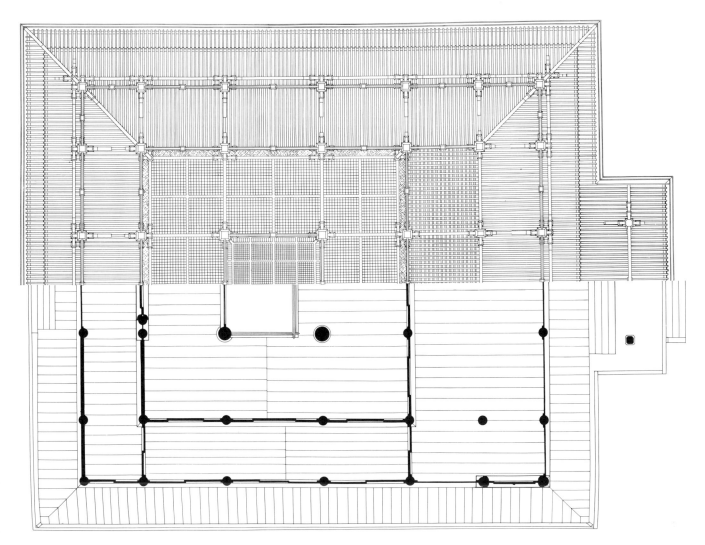

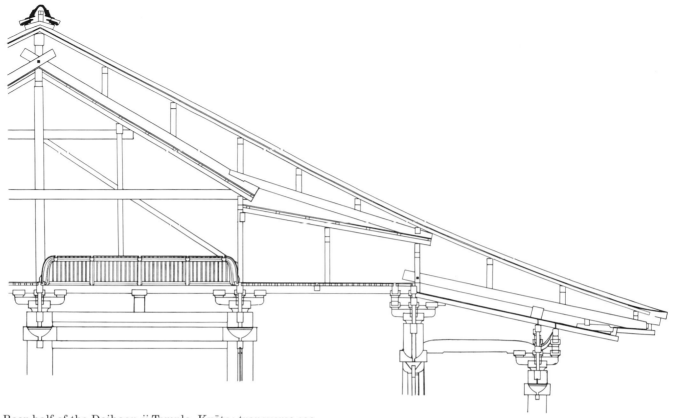

Rear half of the Daihoon-ji Temple, Kyōto: transverse section

girder at the eaves. A little later, in the sixteenth century, a rafter called 'chikara daruki', or 'strong rafter', was used at intervals among the decorative rafters.

At Hōryū-ji, which followed the Chinese prototype, there was a special rafter called 'ōdaruki' supporting the edge beam of the roof, and this idea of supporting deep eaves was probably the prototype of the 'hanegi' and the 'chikara daruki'. This Japanese development of cantilever structure allowed a deeper overhang of the eaves, and made the bracketing system a purely decorative device.

Hondō of the Ishizu-dera Temple: transverse section

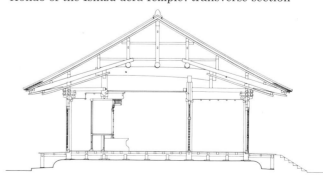

The Block and Bracket System

The ideal dwelling – as described in the Chinese classics – should provide a covered colonnaded space in front of a closed chamber, under one roof. In Japan this same spatial requirement was fulfilled by building a lean-to roof, called a 'hisashi', attached to the columns of the main body of the house, called 'moya', since this was structurally simpler than cantilevering the eaves of the main roof to provide this covered open space. In cantilevered roofs, the eaves rafters normally had to be supported by a girder, called a 'degeta' – or detached girder – at mid-cantilever, which was in turn supported by the bracket system springing from the columns.

The 'masugumi' or block and bracket system was established for this purpose, and can be explained as a series of wooden blocks piled up and corbelling outward. The simplest example, a single bracket, called 'hijiki', balanced on top of a slender square column, occurred in the shrines. In the temples the bracket was supported on a big wooden block, 'daito', which sat on the top of a large circular column. The bracket was called the 'hakari-hijiki', or balanced bracket. The girder was housed in three smaller wooden blocks, 'makito', which were supported by the bracket. This type of block and bracket is called 'hira-mitsudo'. Often another bracket, called the 'sane-hijiki' was housed in the three 'makito' and supported the girder. Sometimes when the block and bracket system was stepped twice, the upper three blocks were supported instead by the ordinary 'hijiki' brachet on a continuous bracket in place of the 'sane-hijiki', called 'tori-hijiki', which was in turn sup-

System of simple blocked brackets (hito-tesaki), Daihoon-ji Temple, Kyōto

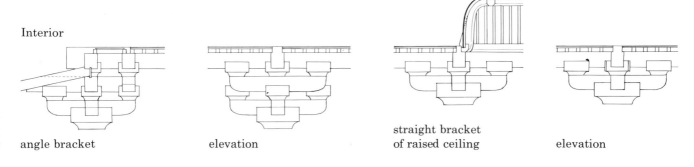

Interior

angle bracket   elevation   straight bracket of raised ceiling   elevation

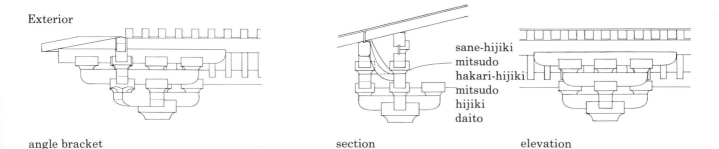

Exterior

angle bracket   section   elevation

sane-hijiki
mitsudo
hakari-hijiki
mitsudo
hijiki
daito

128

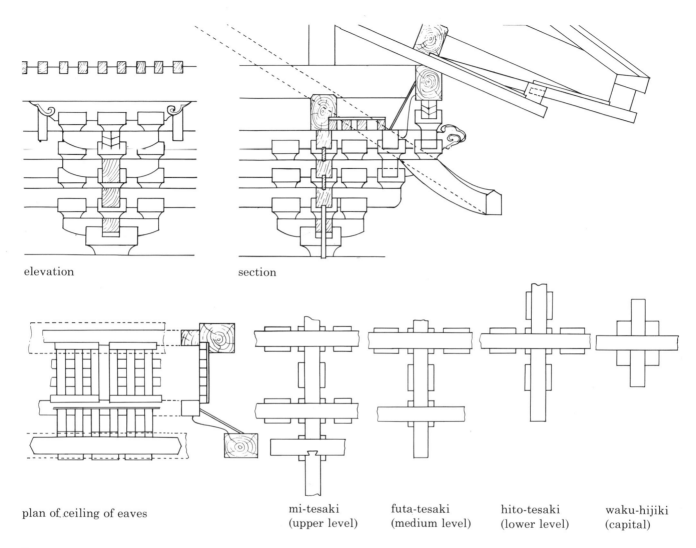

elevation section

plan of ceiling of eaves

mi-tesaki
(upper level)

futa-tesaki
(medium level)

hito-tesaki
(lower level)

waku-hijiki
(capital)

System of triple blocked brackets (mi-tesaki)

ported on the first three 'makito'. In this simple case the blocks and brackets supported the girder, which spanned over the columns in the same plane as the wall. At the corner of the building the 'hakari-hijiki' and the girders crossed over and extended beyond the corner. Blocks on the ends of the brackets supported the ends of the girders, called 'kibana'. A diagonal bracket at the corner, called 'sumi-hijiki', and a block on its end, called 'nobeto', supported the 'sumiki', or hip rafter. However, as this diagonal corner block did not line up with the other 'makito' blocks, it was sometimes shaped so that the square base on the diagonal bracket changed to a square top with its sides parallel to the other blocks. In this case the corner block is called 'sumito', 'kikuto' or 'onito'.

In a system called 'hito-tesaki', or 'degumi', the big block, or 'daito', resting on top of the column, supports two brackets, one at a right angle, and the other parallel to the wall, which are seated into each other over the 'daito'. This set of brackets is called the 'waku-hijiki', with 'makito' blocks at the ends of the brackets and a block, called 'hoto', at the point of intersection. This 'hoto' block became square only after the fourteenth century. The block which rested on the end of the 'waku-hijiki' projecting outside the building under the eaves, supported another block and bracket again called the 'hakari-hijiki'. The three blocks on this 'hakari-hijiki' supported the detached girder. The blocks and brackets at the corners of the eaves in the 'degumi' system were constructed on the same principle as the hira-mitsudo, described above, but in this case the three outside 'makitos' on the 'hakari-hijiki' supported the 'gagyō', or detached girder. The 'hakari-hijiki' were crossed over at the corner, as were the 'gagyō', and the intersection of the 'hakari-hijiki' supported by the 'onito' block on the 'sumi-hijiki', the diagonal corner bracket.

'Futa-tesaki', a double bracket protruding from the wall, and 'mi-tesaki', a triple bracket protruding from the wall, were constructed on the same principle, but in these cases the block on the end of the 'waku-hijiki' at right angles to the wall supported only a bracket called 'tsunagi-hijiki', also projecting from the wall. The 'hakari-hijiki', or balanced bracket was supported on a block at the end of the 'tsunagi-hijiki' (see illustration).

In the construction of the 'mi-tesaki', the detached girder rested on a 'sane-hijiki' bracket which was supported by three blocks on the detached 'hakari-hijiki'. This 'hakari-hijiki' was supported by a block resting on the 'odaruki', a special rafter positioned over a block resting on the 'odaruki', a special rafter positioned over each column. The 'odaruki' was supported at its midpoint by a block on the 'tsunagi-hijiki'. Including this last block there were three blocks, or 'makito', on the 'hakari-hijiki' which crossed each other, with the 'tsunagi-hijiki', on the

same level, while the blocks supported the 'tori-hijiki' or a girder.

All triple bracket systems, or 'mi-tesaki', employed the 'sumi-hijiki', a bracket extending diagonally from the corner. By the tenth century the techniques for finishing the bracket details at the corner had been perfected, and the 'sane-hijiki', which supported the detached girder, crossed regularly, at the corners, over a block on the diagonal 'odaruki' called the 'sumi-odaruki' (see illustration). Prior to this there was some confusion in the construction of the blocks and brackets at the corner.

There were two ways of constructing a corner in the 'mi-tesaki' system. If the distance between the blocks on the 'tsunagi-hijiki' and the block on the 'odaruki' were made sufficiently large, the 'hakari-hijiki' on the 'odaruki' nearest the corner would not cross over on the diagonal, but would be independent. Otherwise all the dimensions of the positions of the blocks projecting from the wall had to be coordinated with that of the block on the 'odaruki', making it possible to make a compact system at the corner, where the brackets joined over the diagonal 'sumi-hijiki' in the 'futa-tesaki' and the 'mi-tesaki' positions, and the 'sane-hijiki' which supported the crossed detached girders (see illustrations).

The Hōō-dō of the Byōdō-in is the oldest example of a perfected 'mi-tesaki' bracket system. In this case there were two diagonal corner 'sumi-odaruki', one above the other. The higher one projected out from between the intersection of the joined 'sane-hijiki' and that of the 'hakari-hijiki'. The purpose of the higher 'odaruki' was to support the 'sumi-ki', the hip rafter, by a small post standing on the end of the higher 'odaruki'. The junction of the 'hakari-hijiki' was supported by a block on the end of the lower 'sumi-odaruki'. The 'sumi-ki' was constructed in two parts, the 'ji-sumiki' or primary hip rafter, and the 'hien-sumiki', the secondary hip rafter, above it (see illustration).

The typical form of the 'mi-tesaki' block and bracket system thus had four ends of diagonal corner members, the two 'sumi-odaruki' and above them the 'ji-sumiki' and the 'hien-sumiki'.

The most complicated and organic form of block

System of triple blocked brackets (mi-tesaki): angle treatment

The topmost bracket, the free girder and the jack rafter

futa-tesaki (medium level)

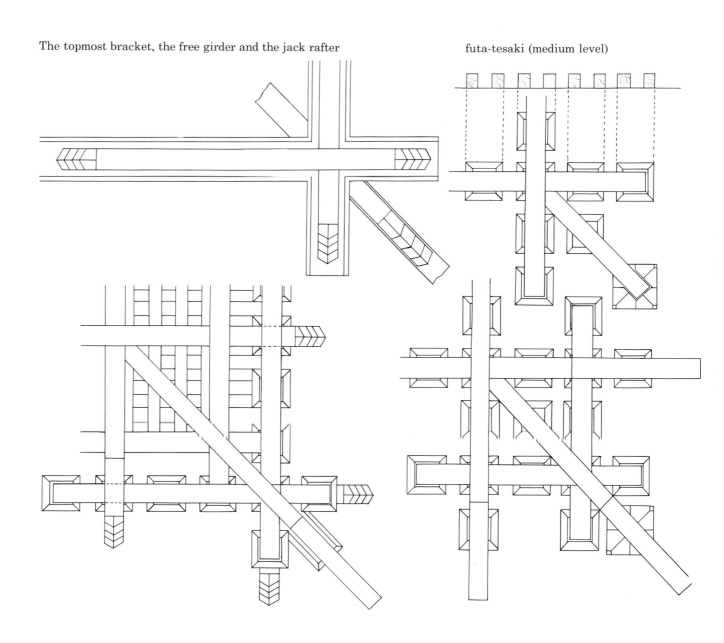

mi-tesaki (upper level)

mi-tesaki seen from below

and bracket system at the corner was technically perfected by the end of the eleventh century, when the brackets still had a structural function and the 'keshō-yane' was supported by girders which rested on the brackets. The 'keshō-yane' supported the 'no-yane', or real rafters, by posts and purlins above it. The 'hanegi' cantilever between the two roofs was not invented until the early thirteenth century, and, with its adoption, the block and bracket system became merely a decorative traditional symbol in the temple.

The girders above the columns, and the detached girders at mid-cantilever in the eaves, 'gagyō' or 'degeta', running along the four sides of a hipped or similar roof, were at right angles to the visible rafters. But where the ends of these girders crossed over at the corners of the building they became parallel to the rafters. If, as was desirable for visual reasons, the extensions of these girders beyond the corner were to occur above the centre line between two adjacent rafters, then the distance between the two girders was defined by the distance from the centre line of the wall and the girder above it, to the block which supported the detached girder. Thus the block and bracket system had to be coordinated with the rafter spacing, centre to centre, called 'shi'. As the rafter spacing was based on the spacing of the columns, to achieve the complete coordination of all the details the whole structure had to be based on the module 'shi'. This modular system called 'shi-wari' was not completely coordinated with the column spacing until the middle of the thirteenth century. At Fudō-dō of Kongōbu-ji, 1197, and the main hall of Daihōon-ji, 1227, attempts were made to achieve this complete coordination, and it was realized in the main hall of Honsan-ji in 1300. From the beginning of the fourteenth century it was the guiding principle of temple design.

A complete modular coordination called 'roku-shi-kake' was established in the main hall of the Taizan-ji, 1305, and in other buildings in the earlier half of the fourteenth century. In this system the centre to centre dimension between two adjacent rafters, 'shi', was common for the four sides of the temple; the distance between the detached girder and the girder over the columns was coordinated with the 'shi' module. The total length of three blocks on one bracket was equal to the distance between the outer faces of six of the spaced rafters, the length of each block on the bracket was equal to the distance between the outer faces of two of the spaced rafters, and the distance between the blocks on the bracket equal to the distance between the rafters (see illustration).

The problem of coordinating the rafter spacing at the corners of the building, called 'naitsuke-daruki', was not solved until the middle of the fourteenth century. The number of shorter rafters which joined the hip rafter at the corner depended on the depth of the eaves; therefore this dimension had to be coordinated in the module. The depth of the eaves was measured from the centre line of the girder over the columns to the outside face of the rail joining the end of the rafters. This rail was called 'kioi' in the case of a single rafter at the eaves, and 'kayaoi' in the case of a double rafter at the eaves. The double rafter had two rails, the 'kioi' at the end of the primary rafters, and the 'kayaoi' at the end of the secondary rafters at the edge of the eaves. When there was no modular coordination of the eaves' width, the rafters were oddly spaced about the point of intersection of the 'kioi' or 'kayaoi' and the hip rafter. The vertical side of the hip rafter was called the 'kuchi-waki'. In the case of a double rafter, the point of intersection of the centre-line of the outside face of the 'kioi' and the hip rafter was called the 'ronji', and it was most important that this point should be properly coordinated with the rafter spacing. Since the secondary rafters – 'hien-taruki' – were in line with the primary rafters, 'ji-taruki', if the point of 'ronji' was not carefully placed, the intersection of the two rafters, the 'kioi' and the hip rafter, became very confused. Later on, when this method of modular coordination was perfected, as for example in the great hall of the Ishuzu-dera temple, 1359, the first shorter rafter of the secondary rafters forming the angle of the temple was centred on the 'ronji' and was called the 'ronji-taruki'. This allowed the precise arrangement of all the double rafters. However the position of 'ronji' was very difficult to determine, since it depended on the depth of the primary rafters, their gradient, the incli-

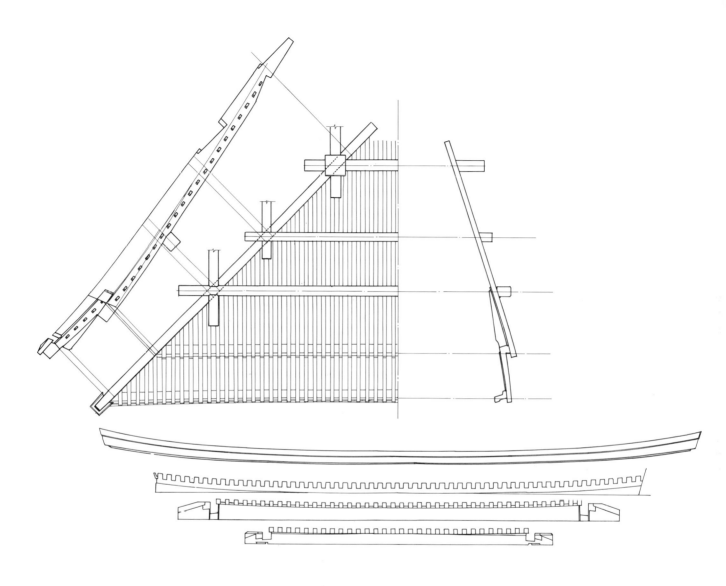

Angle of the eaves of the Sanmyō-ji Temple: detail

nation of the outside face of the 'kioi' to the vertical plane, 'nage-kōbai', the curve of the 'kioi', and the width of the hip rafter. The position of the 'ronji' was marked on the hip rafter on the ground, and could only be determined precisely with the introduction of the carpenter's square, as we shall see later.

The End of the Eaves

Another problem in the design of the eaves was the upcurved ends. The curve was defined by the point at which the eaves began to curve, the height of the corner of the eaves above this point, and the geometric nature of the curve. This point of initial curvature determined the horizontal length of the curve. When it coincided with the centre line of the building the whole eaves were curved, called 'shin-sori'. These three factors, the height, the point of initial curvature, and the nature of the curve could be chosen for the desired visual effect. But because of the technical difficulties involved, simple curves such as circles, elipses and parabolas, or a combination of them were chosen.

The primary rafters were joined at one point to the detached girder, or the girder over the columns, and at the end to the 'kioi'. The secondary rafters were joined to the 'kioi' and the 'kayaoi'. The cross-section of each rafter in a curving eave was a different parallelogram, because the upper and lower faces had to be parallel to the tangent of the curve, while the sides had to remain vertical for the whole eave. Therefore when the top of the girder was not parallel with the curve of the 'kioi', the upper and lower face of each primary rafter had to be twisted. The same was true for the secondary rafters if the curves of the 'kioi' and the 'kayaoi' were not parallel. The position of the rafters on the curve, and the length of each rafter, had to be determined on the ground, and it thus became nearly impossible to make these rafters precisely. The slightest variation due either to poor workmanship or warping, was readily apparent. To minimize this problem the girders were also curved at the ends, and either the columns were gradually decreased in length or the grooves of the blocks were gradually decreased in depth towards the corners of the building. This was usual practice from ancient times until the construction of the Kondō – at Onjō-ji – in 1599. A simpler method, used in gable roofs, was to curve only the top of the girder, and this method later became generally popular with carpenters because of its simplicity, after the construction of the Tenhorin-dō of Enryaku-ji in 1347.

The simplest way to solve all these problems was to make the curves of the top of the girder over the columns, that of the detached girder, the 'kioi', and the 'kayaoi', the same or parts of the same curve. The longest curved member was the 'kayaoi', and once its curve had been established, the curves of the 'kioi',

the top of the detached girder, and that of the girder over the columns, would be progressively smaller parts of the same curve, with a common point of initial curvature. This could be achieved by using a template to define the curve.

The 'kioi' and 'kayaoi', the rails which joined the ends of the primary and secondary rafters, were curved by shaping the top and bottom. The sides were straight. But since these rails were inclined to the vertical they gradually became further away from the wall towards the corner of the building (see illustration). If the outer faces of the two rails were not parallel, then they diverged from the centre point at a different rate and resulted in each secondary rafter joining the two rails being a different length. To avoid this difficulty the outer face of the 'kioi' and the 'hayaoi' had to be parallel despite the different gradients of the primary and secondary rafters.

All these techniques were accomplished by the early sixteenth century in the three storied pagoda of Sanmyō-ji, 1531 (see illustration).

After the development of the real hidden structure in the fourteenth century, the carpenters and their chiefs concentrated on the development of a precise modular system for the visible imitation structure under the eaves. This structure freed from the restriction of having to support the roof, could be developed as a sophisticated aesthetic expression of structure.

Plates

Katsura, Detached Villa (Kyōto)

139 The Ko-Shoin, the oldest building, Chū-Shoin, and Shin-Shoin, the newest building, step diagonally back toward left to afford a view of the garden from each of them.

140 From the right, the Ko-Shoin, Chū-Shoin, and Shin-Shoin, and the boat landing in the garden.

141 The steps of the covered veranda of the Ko-Shoin.

142 The stepping stones at the junction of various passages in the moss of the entrance court.

143 The entrance and stepping stones.

144 Looking under the veranda at the juncture of the Chū-Shoin and the innermost Shin-Shoin.

145 From the left, the Shin-Shoin, the covered veranda, and the Chū-Shoin.

146 The interior of the Ko-Shoin.

147 The Shōkin-tei, a pavilion in the garden.

148 In Shōkin-tei, showing the service facilities in the covered open space, the 'hisashi'.

149 The interior of Shōkin-tei pavilion.

Tai-an, Myōki-an (Kyōto Prefecture)

150 The entry of the tea-room, the Tai-an.

151 Tokonoma of Tai-an, the tea-room designed by Sen-no-Rikyū.

Mittan, Daitoku-ji (Kyōto)

152–153 The tea-room in one of the priest quarters.

Ryōkaku-tei, Ninna-ji (Kyōto)

154 The pavilion in the garden, a rest house with a small tea-room, in the Sukiya-zukuri. This style is free of any formal demands, and is more concerned with the creation of a delicate spatial feeling; it allows more liberty to the tastes of the owner or designer.

155 The veranda and exterior of the tea-room.

Bōsen, Kōhō-an, Daitoku-ji (Kyōto)

156 The passage at the front of the Bōsen, the guest room, to the Buddha Hall.

157 The same passage with shōji-screen, and the garden, seen from within Bōsen.

Ryōkaku-tei, Ninni-ji (Kyōto)

158 Mizuya in the back and Hiroma in the front.

159 The fusuma, or sliding doors of the 'tana', the built-in cabinet, are covered with gilt.

Yoshimura House (Ōsaka Prefecture)

160 The rural house was built at the beginning of the Edo Period. The plan includes private rooms, a guest room, and working space with a floor of beaten earth.

161 Detail of the veranda of the private park.

162 The beaten earth floor inside the entry, which also was the working space. Beyond is the kitchen.

163 Paper-covered sliding doors of rooms and storage closets.

Hase-dera (Nara Prefecture)

164 The settlement in front of Hase-dera.

Kiso-Kaidō (Nagano Prefecture)

165 A settlement in the Kiso Valley.

Jōri-sei settlement (Nara Prefecture)

166 One of the typical villages in the Yamato basin. The rectangular allotment of land, called Jōri-sei, gave the settlement a basic grid pattern.

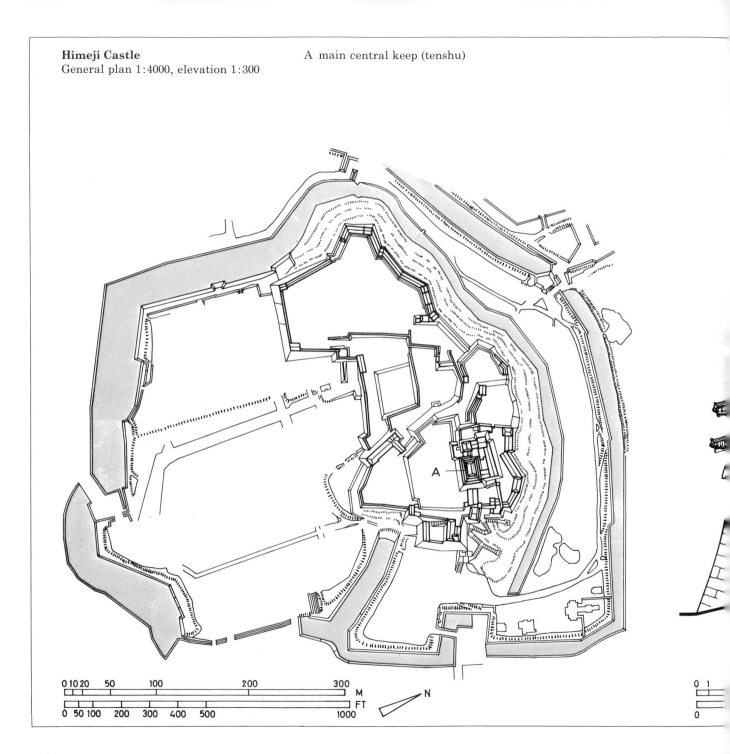

Himeji Castle
General plan 1:4000, elevation 1:300

A main central keep (tenshu)

0 10 20   50   100   200   300   M
0 50 100   200   300   400   500   1000   FT

N

0 1
0

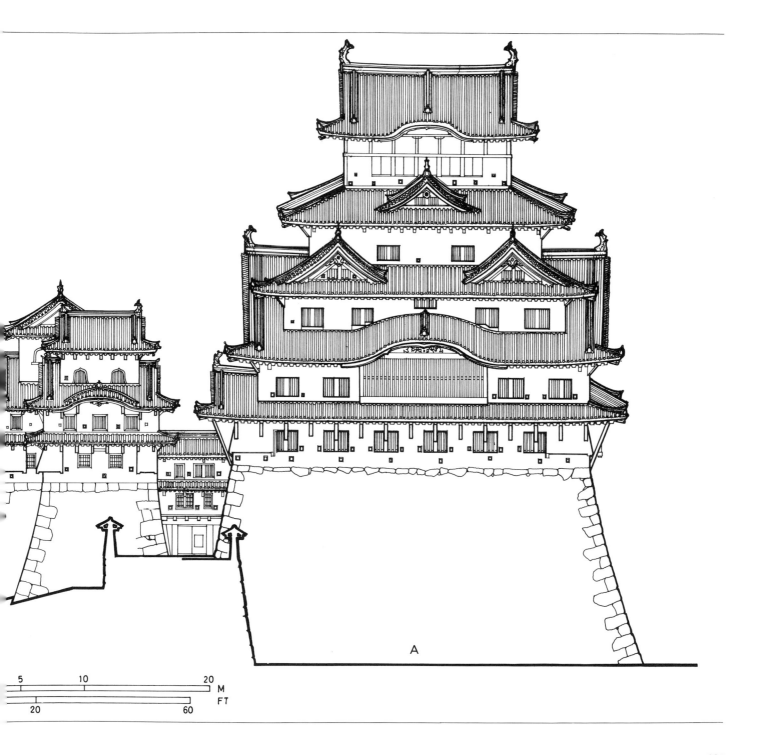

A

5　　　　10　　　　　　　20
|————|————————————| M
　20　　　　　　　　60 FT

Notes

(Continuation from p. 100.)

Assume that AC is the inclination of a hip rafter in a hipped roof in the next diagram.

If AB = 1 shaku, then the length of BC = kōbai of the hip rafter AC. The length of BD = chūkō-kōbai of AC = the kōbai of KL. This means that the inclination of the upper face in the cross section of the hip rafter can be read on the diagram directly, drawn on a side of the hip rafter.

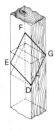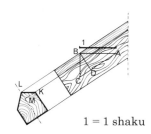

1 = 1 shaku

The chōgen-kōbai and tangen-kōbai are used to draw the ends of members which are inclined to the horizontal, the vertical, or to both, that is, DEFG in the above diagram.

The square can, of course, be used to draw simple joints of members intersecting at right angles – beam and column, for example – but through use of various kind of inclinations, kōbai, it can also be used to draw the joints of members which intersect at angles other than 90°, curved members and members inclined to the vertical. For example, using

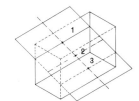

1 = denaka-shin
2 = honnaka-shin
3 = irinaka-shin

the omotome scale of the short arm and the urame scale on the reverse side of the long arm, the carpenter could draw

the hypotenuse of a right triangle projected onto another plane inclined at 45°. Thus, he could draw the slope of a rafter on the lateral face of the hip rafter.

When drawing the positions of the joints directly on the face of a member, the carpenter had to consider the thickness of the member. It was necessary to comprehend the different axes of the members. The intersection of the axes of two members was called the honnaka-shin. The point of intersection of the axis of a member intersecting the near side of another member was called irinaka-shin, and the point of intersection of this axis with the far side of the member was called denaka-shin.

The simplest use of the carpenter's square for drawing joints on the timber was to find the intersection of the vertical plane of the side face of the hip rafter, the kuchiwaki, with the plane of the outer face of the kayaoi, which is inclined to the vertical. This line of intersection of the two planes was called the nagesumi of the kayaoi at the kuchi-waki.

The point G and the vertical through G, the tatemizu have been predetermined. The inclination of the outer face of the kayaoi to the vertical, that is; the hage-kōbai of AC, is chosen by the designer and therefore known. Then the required line can be found if the carpenter's square is set with the long arm such that IG = ½ shaku in urame and the short arm such that IH is at the inclination of the outer face of the kayaoi, measured on the omote scale.

It was then only necessary to construct the vertical line, tatemizu, through the single application of the square, to draw the inclination of the outer face of the kayaoi on the side face of the hip rafter using the carpenter's scale.

Using the same principle many more complex joints could be drawn. This tool and its technique were invaluable in developing the precise and regular timber details of Japanese architecture.

153

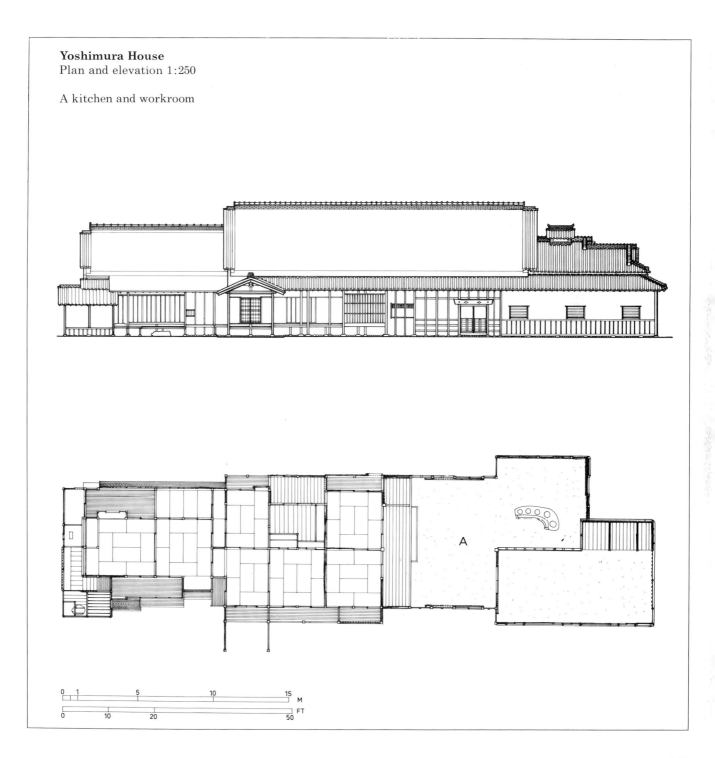

Yoshimura House
Plan and elevation 1:250

A kitchen and workroom

0 1 5 10 15 M
0 10 20 50 FT

Imperial villa, Katsura
General plan 1:400

A tea-pavilion (gepparo)
B oldest building (ko-shoin)
C middle building (chū-shoin)
D most recent building (shin-shoin)

N

0 1   5   10   20   30
                               M
0   10   20   50   100
                               FT

4. Urbanism

The Capital City

The modern Japanese word for capital, 'miyako', originally meant the location of an honorable house, and after the establishment of the Imperial government, it meant the location of the Imperial residence. It was the custom to erect a new Imperial residence when a new emperor was enthroned. One emperor even moved his palace several times during his reign following singular events, both good and bad. This custom can probably be explained by the superstitious nature of the times, or by the system of inheritance on the maternal line.

In 646, the institution of an Imperial capital was imported from China, but the old idea of a transient 'miyako' did not completely disappear. Over a dozen magnificent capitals, which had been constructed or projected with great cost and effort, were removed and rebuilt between the years A.D. 647 and 794, spanning the reigns of ten emperors:

Emperor Kōtoku	646	Naniwa	(Ōsaka)
Empress Saimei	651	Asuka	(South of Nara)
Emperor Tenchi	668	Ōmi	(Ōtsu)
Emperor Tenmu	673	Asuka	(South of Nara, but a little distance from that of 651)
Empress Jitō	694	Fujiwara	(South of Nara)
Empress Gemmyō	710	Heijō	(Nara)
Emperor Seimu	740	Kuni	(North of Nara)
Emperor Seimu	742	Shigaraki	(Shiga Prefecture)
Emperor Seimu	744	Naniwa	(Ōsaka)
Emperor Seimu	745	Heijō	(Nara, reconstructed)
Empress Kōken	761	Hōra: Northern capital	(Shiga Prefecture)
Empress Shōtoku	769	Yūgi: Western capital	(Ōsaka Prefecture)
Emperor Kammu	784	Nagaoka	(Southwest of Kyōto)
Emperor Kammu	794	Heian	(Kyōto)

Heian-kyō, or Kyōto, the last Imperial capital, continued to be the seat of the Imperial aristocracy for over ten centuries, until the Emperor Meiji moved to Tōkyō – called Edo until the end of the Tokugawa Period – in 1869. One of the principal reasons for Heian-kyō's durability as the Imperial capital was the usurpation of the emperors' political power by the aristocracy in the ninth century. With the demise of the Ritsuryō System, and the rise of the Sekkan System in the A.D. 850's, the emperors lost all effective temporal authority, and the location of the capital became fixed.

Although Kyōto – Heian-kyō – remained the titular seat of authority until the Meiji Restoration, the effete court aristocracy gradually lost its political dominance, and the 'miyako' degenerated into a symbolic font of authority, with no true power. Minamoto Yoritomo established the first 'bakufu', or military government, at Kamakura, in 1192. Although Heian-kyō continued to develop as a commercial city, it never regained its former style. Even with the overthrow of the Minamoto and the establishment of a new 'bakufu' in Kyōto by Ashikaga Takauji, in 1366, the old capital did not regain its former significance.

The word 'machi' originally meant one block of cultivated fields. When the capital was laid out on a rectangular grid it also came to mean one city block bounded by four streets.

The east and west markets of the capitals were called 'ichi'. This word originally meant a gathering of people, or a meeting place. Because of the exchange of goods which gradually developed at public meetings the word came to mean trade market.

The city-scape in Japan is a composite of the 'miyako', 'ichi', and 'machi'. Its inhabitants were engaged in secondary industry and not bound to the soil as were the rural population.

The city blocks of Fujiwara-kyō, Heijō-kyō and Heian-kyō were laid out on the model of Ch'ang-an, the T'ang Dynasty capital of China, but the shape of the blocks was influenced by the existing system of land division for rice cultivation, the 'jōri' system. One block in Ch'ang-an, called a 'bō', was a rectangle with its long axis lying east-west, but in Japan the 'bō' were generally square. The provincial capitals, like Dazaifu in northern Kyūshū, Suho, in Hiroshima Prefecture, and Izumo, in Shimane Prefecture, were planned so that the existing 'jōri' land division grid coincided with the 'jō-bō' city grid. Hiraizumi, which was the centre of northeastern Japan in the Heian Era, and Kamakura at the beginning of the mediaeval period, also followed the square grid system. The planners probably imagined this to be the only possible structural pattern for a city.

At Heijō-kyō the plan of the capital was based on the existing 'Yamato jōri' land division system. The ancient central road of the Yamato basin, 'Shimotsu-michi', was adopted as the central road of Heijō-kyō, and the south gate of the city, Rajō-mon', built on it. Thus the city had the same axial plan as the whole basin, and this identification with the regional plan, over 16 miles from north to south, is an important characteristic of the ancient Japanese capital. Spatial organization on a smaller scale was used later very effectively in the borrowed landscape of the Japanese gardens where distant hills were made to seem part of the garden by plantings or walls which concealed other nearby buildings.

Despite the change in the unit of measurement, the pre-existing small unit of land area in the Yamato Basin, the 'tsubo', was used as the basic unit of land measurement in planning the city. The larger pre-existing unit of land division was a square, thirty-six 'tsubo' in area, called 'ri'; a line of 'ri' east and west was called 'jō'. But the large blocks adopted in the city were smaller squares, sixteen 'tsubo' in area, called 'bō'. The original division of land into 'jō' was changed and reorganized as a whole after Heijō-kyō was established. As a result, the 'jō' were staggered with one 'tsubo' displacement in the numbering system to either side of the central road running through the basin. The 'bō' in the city plan were directly in line on either side of the central road. Therefore the city plan did not correspond exactly, except for the central road of the capital, and at the boundaries of the city there was a discontinuity in the block system of the region.

The 'tsubo' were bounded by four narrow streets, and the large unit divisions, the 'bō', were bounded by four wide roads called 'ōji'.

The city plan consisted of eight 'bō' east to west, and nine 'bō' north to south. The central main road was called Sujaku-ōji, and ran from the main gate of the Imperial court, that is, the governmental quarter, including the Imperial palace, which was a large square four 'bō' in area, to the southern main gate of the city. This road divided the city into two equal parts, Sakyō, the left half of the capital, on the west, and Ukyō, the right half of the capital, on the east. The 'bō' were numbered outward from the central road, 1st 'bō', 2nd 'bō', 3rd 'bō', and 4th 'bō', to the east and the west. To fix the position in the north-south direction, this line of four 'bō' was called a 'jō', starting with 1st 'jō' in the north, to 9th 'jō' in the south. Because of this method of naming we call this pattern of urban planning 'Jō-bō' system.

The overall plan of Ch'ang-an in China was a rec-

Plan of the city of Chang'An, capital of China under the T'ang Dynasty

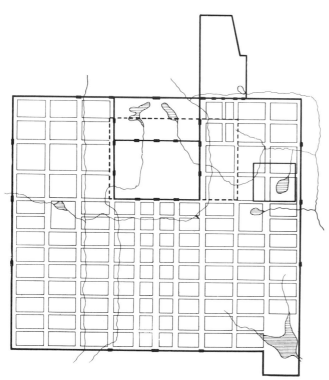

tangle with the long axis pointing east-west, but at Fujiwara-kyō, Heijō-kyō, Nagaoka-kyō, and Heian-kyō the overall plan was a rectangle with the long axis in the north-south direction. The total area of Heijō-kyō, when it was first laid out, was 6667 yards north to south by 4817 yards east to west. However, soon after the capital was transferred the plan was extended in the Sakyō area and an area of twelve 'bō' was added between the 2nd and 5th 'jō', making the plan irregular. The present Nara is located on the eastern part of this extension of ancient Heijō-kyō. Some time later a new Imperial palace was built to the East of the governmental quarter, adjacent to the old palace. This asymmetrical plan is a unique characteristic of the ancient capitals of Japan.

The square 'Jō-bō' system of planning was a mechanical copy of the city plan of Ch'ang-an modified by existing land division systems, and no particular thought was given to the realities of urban life. Generally speaking, the planning of Ch'ang-an in T'ang China was based on the ritual concept that the emperor must face the South, but the allotment of the living quarters was quite rational. The 'bō' in Ch'ang-an, with the exception of those directly to the south of the Imperial court, which were square, were all rectangular, with the long axis pointing east-west. Even the square 'bō' had a single smaller road running through them from east to west making oblong building lots. The rectangular 'bō' were subdivided by smaller crossing roads into four similar oblong blocks, and as a result it was possible to arrange every house facing the sun, and with a courtyard garden. But in Japan even in those 'tsubo' blocks which had few north-south lanes, as in parts of Heian-kyō, the houses faced the main roads bounding the block, as do the more densely built present-day houses in central Kyōto.

The Japanese, unlike the Chinese, had no experience with urban life before the institution of the capital was imported from the continent. Because of the small scale of the topography, and the agricultural livelihood of rice-cultivation in primarily swampy land, large settlements engaged in collective production were not necessary, and settlements rarely numbered more than one family. This lack of urban experience made the capital merely a symbol of political authority and it scarcely functioned as a collective urban society. Most of the inhabitants were governmental officers, often single men who had left their families in the provinces.

In China, capital towns were surrounded by a city wall, but in Japan in the ancient capitals this custom was not followed, or, if it was, the city wall was not large enough to defend the city. The southern city wall of Heian-kyō, 31′ high, was probably for visual effect when approaching the capital. There are no records of the city wall, the width of the roads, and the residential division of one 'tsubo' in Heijō-kyō, but we may partially visualize them as there are such records for ancient Heian-kyō, and these two capitals were of almost the same form and scale. Documents also exist for the official bestowal of residential lots to aristocrats according to rank in Naniwa-kyō and Fujiwara-kyō.

Heian-kyō was established eighty-four years after Heijō-kyō, and only ten years after Nagaoka-kyō, to the south-west of present-day Kyōto. It also had a rectangular plan, nine and a half 'bō' by eight 'bō', as the northern end of the city was extended by half a 'bō'. Its overall dimensions were a rectangle 3.2 miles in the north-south direction by 2.8 miles in the east-west direction. The plan of Ch'ang-an was 6.1 miles east-west by 5.1 miles north-south. Thus the areas of Heian-kyō and Heijō-kyō were about a quarter of the area of Ch'ang-an.

The main central road in Heian-kyō was also called Sujaku-ōji, as at Heijō-kyō. It was 28 'jō' (278 feet) wide. The other roads running east-west and north-south varied from 4 'jō', 40 feet, to 8 'jō', or 12 'jō', to the road south of the 2nd 'Jō' of buildings, which was 17 'jō' wide. The main gate of the Imperial court opened onto this last road. These roads had ditches on both sides which varied from 4 'shaku' to 10 'shaku' wide, and had verges on either side from 5 'shaku' to 7 'shaku' wide. At the southern end of Sujaku-ōji was the Rashō-mon, the main central gate of Heian-kyō.

The Imperial court of Heian-kyō was two 'tsubō', or ½ 'bō', longer in the north direction than that of Heijō-kyō, and its overall dimensions were a rectangle 2.5 'bō', or $^9/_{10}$ mile north to south by 2 'bō', or $^7/_{10}$ mile, east to west. The standard residential lot of the higher aristocrats was one 'chō' or 'machi', that is, one 'tsubo', 400 feet square, and only people of this class were allowed to construct their entrance gates facing the main road. The 'chō' were numbered in each 'bō' from the 1st 'Chō' to the 16th 'Chō'.

The division of land into residential lots for the commoners was called '4 gyō 8 mon'; the 'chō' blocks were divided into four in the east-west direction and into eight in the north-south direction, to form 32 rectangular blocks called 'henushi', and one 'henushi' in area was 10 'jō' by 5 'jō' or about 100 feet by 50 feet. These blocks were numbered from the side nearest the central road either to the east or to the west, 1st 'Gyō', 2nd 'Gyō', etc., and from north to south 1st 'Mon' to 8th 'Mon'. The residential blocks were therefore numbered on a 'Gyō-mon' grid system similar to the 'Jō-bō' system for the large city blocks. Some of the 'chō' had a central lane running from north to south and some also had a cross lane running from east to west, while some had no interior

Plan showing the situations of some ancient capitals

1 Heian-Kyō	4 Shiragaki	7 Fujiwara-Kyō
2 Otsu-Kyō	5 Kuni	8 Naniwa-Kyō
3 Nagaoka-Kyō	6 Heijo-Kyō	

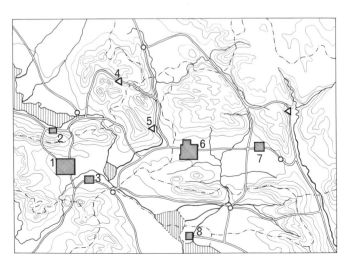

roads. Theoretically therefore a house could be located by its area, 'Sakyō' or 'Ukyō', 'Jō-bō' numbers, 'Chō' number and 'Gyō-mon' numbers. However, in practice the residential lots did not rigidly follow the 'Gyō-mon' system, and judging from medieval picture scrolls the 5 'jō' frontages were further subdivided in actual practice. According to later folding screen paintings, the dwellings of the common people faced roads or lanes to the east, west, north and south, and had an enclosed yard inside.

Altogether, 443 commoner families had moved to Heian-kyō in the century after its origin. They were called 'kyōko'. Some were powerful city families from the former capital, and some were rich people from the country. Many provincial farmers wished to become 'kyōko' since city dwellers were not taxed as the farming class were.

One of the important reasons for the removal of the capital to Heijō-kyō in A.D. 710 had been to express the national power and authority established with the Taika Reforms, as well as to destroy the political power of the families of the Asuka district who had surrounded the former capital.

At Heijō-kyō, to increase the beauty of the capital, the construction of Buddhist temples by both the Imperial family and the aristocrats was encouraged. Buddhism was adopted as the national religion and temples were built all over the country. The great temples which flourished at Heijō-kyō were known as the Seven Great Temples, and resulted in a grand townscape, but it also resulted in political power falling into the hands of the priests. Therefore when Heian-kyō was founded the construction of the temples in the city was forbidden, and at first it was simply the centre of the Ritsuryō government. However, the aristocratic families from Heijō-kyō, who regarded the former capital as their spiritual home, made pilgrimages to the temples there. This was considered politically unwise, and to discourage this practice two official temples were built in Heian-kyō two years after the transfer: Tōji, the East Temple, and Saiji, the West Temple. They were erected just inside the southern main gate on either side of the main central road on the sites which had been reserved as houses for visiting diplomats, based on the

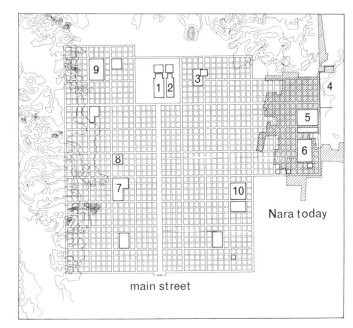

main street

Nara today

1 chōdōin	imperial quarter	6 Gankō-ji Temple
2 dairi		7 Yakushi-ji Temple
3 Hokke-ji Temple		8 Tōshōdai-ji Temple
4 Tōdai-ji Temple		9 Saidai-ji Temple
5 Kōfuku-ji Temple		10 Daian-ji Temple

Plan of Heijo-Kyō

Ch'ang-an precedent.

During the mid-ninth century, in the Sekkan Period, the government was in the hands of the powerful Fujiwara family and a Fujiwara regent ruled in the name of the emperor. Although work on the capital had ceased ten years after the transfer, the Fujiwara family and other aristocrats constructed many elaborate private temples to the east of Heian-kyō, as temples in the city were forbidden. Within the capital, which had never been finished, there still remained rice fields. Their cultivation was encouraged at first but later prohibited. An official document of A.D. 828 records 580 'chō' in Heian-kyō, which was less than half the planned city area of 1,215 'chō'. A similar situation had existed in Ch'ang-an, where there were empty blocks and few houses in the southern 40 'bō' of the capital.

173

Half a century after the transfer of the capital, Ukyō, the western half, had become desolate because the ground was – and still is – damp, especially in the area south of the 4th 'Jō', and south of the 2nd 'Jō' it has clay soil. This part of the capital is only 70 feet above sea level, while the north-eastern end is 177 feet above sea level. Sakyō, on the other hand, was densely populated. It is situated in an alluvial fan-shaped area of the Kamo River in the north-east of Kyōto. The sand and pebble ground was high and dry, and it was also an area of great natural beauty, especially to the east of the Kamo River and along the Shirakawa Creek at the foot of Mt. Higashiyama.

Thus both in Heian-kyō and Heijō-kyō the eastern area, Sakyō, was gradually developed and thickly populated in spite of the plans for a symmetrical capital; in both cases this was caused by people avoiding low lying marsh areas. The natural easterly development of Heian-kyō which resulted in the decline of the formal ritual plan paralleled the decline of the Imperial system of government, the Ritsuryō, and the growth of private ownership of the land and its peasants by powerful landowners, the Shōen System.

In the Kamakura Period the place names in Heian-kyō, which had been numbered according to the 'Jō-bō' block system, began to be called by their names, and in some maps of the period streets were marked both with numbers and names. In the dictionaries of the tenth century, at the end of the Heian Period, the word 'machi' means stalls or shops, but some streets running north-south also became known as 'Machi'. By the early thirteenth century the title deeds were written using the proper names of the street with the 'Jō-bō' block system. At this time, the area between Muromachi Street in the east and Nishi-no-tōin Street in the west was a prosperous commercial centre, and many rows of shops were set up, and the 'Za', a guild system of commerce and manufacture was formed.

These developing areas of Sakyō, the eastern half of the capital, the northern area outside it and the area east of the Kamo River were often damaged by floods, fires and earthquakes, or suffered during rebellions.

The Daigokuden, the central building in the Im-perial court, was burnt down in A.D. 1177 and no records remain of this building. The Emperor Gokomatsu was enthroned in 1392 at the residence of the Fujiwara family called Tsuchimikado-tei, which has been the Dairi or Imperial residence ever since.

During the Ōnin Rebellion, 1467–77, in the late Muromachi Period, more than 30,000 houses were destroyed by fire in the 100 'chō' area which includes the Shirakawa Quarter. This was a fatal disaster for the Imperial city of Heian-kyō, since the reconstruction of the destroyed areas stagnated and the city was divided into two parts. One was called Kami-kyō, the upper city, north of the 1st 'Jō', and the other Shimo-kyō, downtown, between 3rd 'Jō' and 5th 'Jō'. Kami-kyō was inhabited by the decadent aristocrats, who had no authority except in the field of traditional culture, the warriors, and the newly risen wealthy merchant class. Shimo-kyō was the quarter of the middle-class merchants, the craftsmen and the common people.

Kami-kyō was later burned down by Oda Nobunaga, in 1573, but the distinctive townscape of Kami-kyō continued, after its reconstruction, until the end of the recent period. These areas continued to be called old 'kyō', or old town, in spite of the new buildings and increased population.

Nobunaga repaired the Dairi, or Imperial palace, in 1570. Toyotomi Hideyoshi built the Sentō-gosho, the palace for the ex-emperor, and in 1587 erected a magnificent residence for himself called Jūrakudai in the south-eastern portion of the original Imperial court. He then tried to restore Sakyō to its former glory by taking the square 'chō' to the east of Takakura and south of Oshi-no-kōji which was in the east end of the capital and was lying waste, and dividing it into two rectangular blocks by making a lane from north to south, probably basing his plan on ancient documents. He then gathered the medieval temples of various sects which had been built in the city despite the ancient prohibition of constructing temples in the capital and moved them all into areas in the east end and in Kita-aguin, the north end. The areas were named Tera-machi, the temple street, and Tera-no-uchi, temple quarter. He offered the huge old Higashi-ichi site, the eastern market, south of the

Heian-Kyō: original plan
Odoi: earth rampart built by Hideyoshi

Sengoku period (late 15th c.)

Toyotomi Hideyoshi period (early 17th c.)

Tokugawa period (17th and 18th c.)

1 Kinkaku-ji Temple
2 Daitoku-ji Monastery
3 Shimogamo Shinto shrine
4 Ginkaku-ji Temple
5 River Kamo
6 Nanzen-ji Temple
7 Kiyomize-dera Temple
8 Tō-ji Temple

Development of the city of Kyōto

Shimo-kyō downtown area, to the Honganji temple. Tokugawa Ieyasu later offered a site to the Higashi-hongan-ji temple, the Eastern Honganji, and this led to the development of these areas as temple quarters. Hideyoshi also built an earthen rampart, called the 'Odoi', 15 miles long on the west bank of the Kamo River in the east, through the Takagamine Hill in the north, along the Kamiya River in the west, and along the 9th 'Jō' in the south. The city of Heian-kyō then acquired the form of a walled castle town. It was still called Miyako, Imperial capital, but in reality it was already a commercial city.

The construction of a canal, in 1611, called Higashi-takase-gawa which connected Kyōto directly to Ōsaka improved the transport system between the two cities. Before that time Kyōto had depended on supplies from the port of Yodo-no-tsu to the South of the city. As Ōsaka gradually became the foremost commercial centre of Japan, many warehouses were built along the canal, and trading streets grew up, for example Kiya-machi, firewood street, Zaimoku-chō, timber mill street, Sendō-chō, boatman's street, and Komeya-chō, rice shop street.

The population of ancient Heijō-kyō is estimated to have been about 200,000 people; 160,000 men and 40,000 women. This disproportion was due to the large number of single men who came from the country to work as government officers. As mentioned already the west half of Heian-kyō, Ukyō, had always been largely uninhabited, and Heijō-kyō had also been sparsely populated. Judging from old documents they had nearly the same population. However, in the late Medieval Period the population of Kyōto had grown from 300,000 to 500,000, but directly after the transfer of the capital to Tōkyo in 1869 it decreased to 240,000.

The Station Settlements

In the Taika Reform Edict of A.D. 645 the institution of station settlements, 'eki', was ordered along the main roads in Japan for the first time, and horses, belonging to both the central and local governments were kept and raised there under government supervision. Twenty horses were reserved at each station along the most important roads, ten horses at each station along other main roads, and five horses at the stations of the more minor roads.

The most important road in Heian Era was the Sanyōdō, which had 26 stations or stages, between Kyōto and Dazaifu, the provincial capital in Kyūshū.

The most important highways were the 'Tōsandō', which had 61 stages between Kyōto, and the eastern military outpost, and the 'Tōkaidō', which had 46 stages between Kyōto and the seat of the Hitachi provincial government. The minor roads were the 'Hokurikudō', to the north-east of Kyōto, the 'Sanindō' to the north-west of Kyōto, the 'Nankaidō' in Shikoku, the 'Seikaidō' in Kyūshū, the 'Dewaji' in the eastern district of Honshū, the 'Iseji' in Ise, 'Mimasakaji' across the Chūgoku district, the 'Hidaji' in Hida, the 'Kaiji' in Kai, the 'Kazusaji' in the Kantō Plain, the 'Yamatoji' in Yamoto, and the 'Igaji' in Iga.

The stages along these roads were 30 'ri', about 20 kilometres apart, and consisted of stables and rest-houses which were used by travellers on government missions. There were only nine stages in all Japan in the eighth century which provided accommodation for private travellers. The practice of allowing local governments to raise horses for their own use at the stage settlements was abolished in 792, but later, in 927, the custom was revived under the supervision of the central government.

In the Genpei Period, in the latter half of the twelfth century, inns appeared sporadically, and at some stages there were also brothels. In the Kamakura Period, the 'Tōkaidō' road became the most important road because of the location of the government, some stages along it grew prosperous, and inns and brothels appeared.

Oda Nobunaga repaired and widened the 'Tōkaidō' main road to 3.5 'ken', about 23 feet and the 'Tōsandō' to 3 'ken', about 20 feet. He also revised the land measurement system such that 1 'ri' = 36 'chō', instead of the former 1 'ri' = 6 'chō', and as a sign at 1 'ri' intervals along the roads built cairns planted with pine or hackberry trees. The width of the minor roads in the feudal territorial counties was 2 'ken', about 13 feet.

Toyotomi Hideyoshi also attached importance to maintaining the road system, and Tokagawa Ieyasu continued the policy. For the convenience of government messengers and feudal lords who made periodic journeys to Edo, he stabled 100 horses and their riders at every stage on the 'Tōkaidō', 50 horses and riders at every stage on the 'Nakasendō', 25 horses and riders at every stage on the 'Nikkōkaidō', the 'Oshukaidō' in the north-eastern district, and on the 'Kōshukaidō'. Later in some stages free and homeless men acted as private riders, or became thieves. He also planted rows of pines along the main roads so that, as well as the mount every 'ri', called 'chiri zuka', all main arteries in Japan were bordered with trees.

The feudal lords, 'daimyō', on their journeys between their territories and Edo, were at first simply accompanied by a troop of armed soldiers, but later these journeys became grand, luxurious processions, with vast amounts of baggage carried by the men and horses of the stage settlements. The institution of 'sukegō' arose, under which farmers offered their temporary help in carrying the lords' – and other travellers' – equipment in return for exemption from feudal duties. As well as the 'daimyō' processions, there was much traffic along the roads, of peddlers, pilgrims, delivery of tea-jars from the growing areas to Edo, diplomatic missions, etc. Cheap lodging houses were built, which later developed into inns, equipped with baths and tended by servant girls. The stage settlement began to take on the appearance of the recent townscape.

By the early nineteenth century, Goyu, a stage town on the 'Tōkaidō', boasted 316 houses, 4 'honjin' – formal inns to accommodate the 'daimyō' processions – and 62 common inns. In 1800 Shimosuwa, the terminus of the 'Kōshukaidō', which ran through the central mountain district from Edo, was built up along the road for over ½ mile; the width of the road in the settlement varied from 15 to 21 feet, and there were 220 houses, and 42 common inns, as well as 'honjin' and 'wakihonjin', the minor 'honjin'. There was a population of 394 men and 374 women.

The early Edo Period was a time of rapid commercial development, and such settlements as stage towns and market towns prospered throughout Japan in the early half of the nineteenth century. Originally these towns were formed spontaneously, as were the villages, and developed in a linear form along the roads.

At Koaraimachi, in northern Matsu, markets had

been held on three specified days each month since ancient times, and by the early seventeenth century the town numbered 296 houses, which spread to a width of over 650 feet, for 1000 yards along the length of the highway. The houses were built along the sides of the main country road. The northern part of the town was called 'Uemachi', upper street, the middle part 'Nakamachi', middle street, and the southern part 'Shimomachi', lower street.

Muikamachi, in Echigo Province, was situated along the 'Mikunikaidō', and on either side of the road there were 274 houses. To a width of over $1/8$ mile, along 1100 yards of the road's length. 'Muika' means the sixth day, and on the 6th, 16th and 26th of the month a market was held in the town.

According to an account of a trip through Japan in the Edo Period, by a German named Thunberg, the longitudinal dimension of most of the stage settlements and rural towns – that is, their road frontage – was remarkably uniform throughout Japan. The rural towns had several streets running lengthwise, and consisted of merchants, workers, and a considerable number of peasants in houses built in dense rows. By the end of the eighteenth century, especially in the south-west, some of these rural towns had prospered, and many houses had clay tile roofs. The stage settlements, on the other hand, usually had only a single through road, but they were also called 'machi', or town, perhaps because of their urban townscape and size.

The Market Town

A group of shops has been called a 'machi' since the tenth century. This word was used for both the government markets and free trading areas, where there were many shopstalls. The word also came to mean a street, with shops on either side.

The trading streets of Heian-kyō prospered because of the decline of government control over the markets. Also, with the remarkable progress of mediaeval agriculture, there was a good deal of surplus produce for sale. Craftsmen who had worked for the central and local governments in ancient times transferred their allegiance to strong landlords, and estab-lished a guild system to organize private trade for their own products.

During the wars of the fourteenth century, transporting tax goods to the capital became dangerous and difficult, and the system of money payments was widely adopted using Chinese and Japanese coins. This system spread from the Kantō, in the east, to northern Kyūshū, in the west. Along the main roads, in this area, linear settlements developed as the collection and distribution markets for crops. They were similar to the ancient market villages, the port towns, and stage towns, and the markets which grew in front of the famous shrines and temples on festival occasions. In the Middle Ages they all consisted of stores, warehouses, wholesale shops, inns and pawnshops.

One can trace the development of market towns in Japan from the example of the villages once related to the old Suwa Shrine, which were located in the small basin in southern Shinano Province. This basin is triangular, bounded by hills to the north, mountains to the south, and Lake Suwa to the west. It was sparsely settled and had two markets. One, Itsukaichi, opened on the 5th, 15th and 25th days of each month, and the other, Tōkaichi opened on the 10th, 20th and 30th of the month. These markets served not only the Shinano Basin area, but also the priests and pilgrims of the Suwa Shrine, as they were situated at the junction of the roads to the Kōfu, Shinano, and Kiso districts. Prior to the ancient Heian Period there were only two peasant settlements, but by the fifteenth century there were about twenty settlements in the basin although it was only about $2-1/2$ miles wide. These settlements centred around the small towns in front of Suwa Shrine, and about half of these were called 'machi'. The towns in front of shrines or temples were generally called 'Monzen-machi', and in this case had residential quarters for the Shintō priests, inns for pilgrims, souvenir shops, wayside booths in the ancient market places, and stations for the transport of goods and people. This mediaeval urban development was never conceived as a single planned town like Heian-kyō, but consisted of a cluster of expanding individual settlements. At the end of the Middle Ages, castle towns were estab-lished in each district as the seat of local power, and the economic activity of the mediaeval market settlement was transferred to the new castle town. As a result, in the Suwa Basin only the small town at the front of Suwa Shrine remained. The market towns disappeared, and the settlements reverted to mere peasant villages; only their names remained to reflect their former function.

The feudal lords could construct their own towns at will as the ancient emperors had done. Their castle towns took over the trade function of the mediaeval market towns, and when they were made the centres of local government they had both a political and a commercial character. Besides these castle towns the feudal towns were of two types. The older settlements of the ports and markets in front of shrines and temples had survived through the change in political power, such as Nara, Kyōto, Iwashimizu and Yamada, which were temple or shrine markets, and Ōtsu, Kizu, Tsuruga, Yamasaki, Hyōgo and Hakata, which were ports. The new settlements had grown up naturally in the fourteenth century, located also near a shrine or temple, or at a major road junction or waterway. They generally did not have a compact form, but developed linearly along the roads or coast, and became the trade centres of their districts, selling local agricultural or industrial products, as well as grain from the cultivation of new lands in the feudal period.

All these towns, both the new feudal ones, and those ancient ones which had survived, were controlled by the feudal lords or powerful families, and their prosperity depended on the wealth and power of their rulers. As local rulers were defeated in battle and several areas were unified by a stronger lord, most of the towns in front of shrines and temples, which had been so prosperous during the middle ages, lost their function and disappeared. Only those religious centres of national significance such as Nara, Ujiyamada, Nikkō, Itsukushima, and Usa continued to flourish until modern times.

Existing side by side with the natural market towns were the castle towns constructed under direction of the feudal lords. These were a completely new concept in the history of Japanese urban development.

The Castle Town

The history of the castle town corresponds to the history of the castle, and can be divided into three stages. The first stage is from the first half of the fourteenth century until unification under Oda Nobunaga, one of the strongest war lords, in 1576. The second stage is the period from this unification until 1615, when the Tokugawa government ordered the destruction of nearly all the castles in Japan. In the third stage, after this decree, those feudal lords who were admitted to the Tokugawa government systems constructed their own castle towns as the seats of local government.

In the fourteenth century, one of the strongest vassals of the Muromachi 'Bakufu' was the Ōuchi clan. This family transferred its residence from its native settlement of Ōuchi to Yamaguchi, and constructed a new city, comparable to Kyōto at the time, which held markets several times each month. It had many joiners' shops and blacksmiths' forges, and the markets were crowded with bargaining people. Re-

Plan of the fortified town of Takata (Niigata Prefecture) as it was in the 17th century

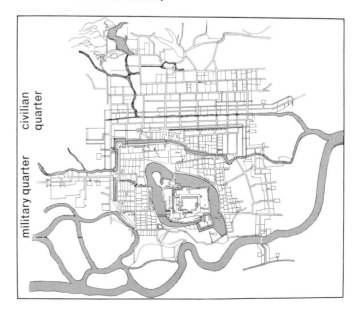

military quarter — civilian quarter

178

ports of the time describe it as a very noisy city. After the defeat of the Ōuchi family, in 1551, the city declined.

The head of the Nagao clan of Echigo founded his castle three miles to the south-west of his residential settlement. This castle, and the Odawara castle of the Hōjō family, were the two biggest castles in existence at the end of the Middle Ages. In the residential settlement called Funai there were about 6,000 houses, and at the foot of the castle, in the market settlement called 'Monzen-machi', about 3,000 houses. Almost all of them had thatched roofs, and the lord ordered that they be changed to wooden board roofs. The same change was made at Odawara. Perhaps the lords wished to make their towns resemble Kyōto, although the regular grid planning of the capital could not be applied in the restricted sites near the castle hill.

In 1576, Oda Nobunaga constructed a castle with a seven-story gilded keep atop Azuchi Hill, to the east of Lake Biwa, and dwelling quarters for warriors, merchants and craftsmen at the foot of the hill. This was the beginning of the second stage of castle construction and the first appearance of the planned castle town. Because the earlier castles had been forts with houses enclosed by a ditch, they could not be regarded as towns.

Greater importance was attached to the workers and craftsmen than to the merchants in the earlier castle towns, because of their military function. They were paid a salary by the feudal lord. Many of the workers came from farmers' villages, so the number of men in the towns usually exceeded the number of women, as at ancient Heijō-kyō.

In the Azuchi castle-town, more merchants than craftsmen were invited to live in the town. These merchants, as well as the craftsmen, were freed from the mediaeval guild system and exempted from taxation in both goods and money by the warlords. The old mediaeval system of commerce through trade trusts and markets was broken down, and the merchants enjoyed a privileged position in the castle towns, which prospered greatly. Castle sites on flat plains or low hills, which enabled the growth of big towns around the castle, became popular.

Nobunaga was succeeded by his vassal, Toyotomi Hideyoshi, who constructed the castle and town of Ōsaka in 1583, with an eight-story keep dominating the town. The castle enclosure was seven miles in circumference, and surrounded by a ditch. To make the town prosperous, some of the influential civilians of Kyōto, Fushimi, Tennōji and Sakai were forcibly transferred to Ōsaka.

In February 1603, Tokugawa Ieyasu, who succeeded Hideyoshi, began to make projects for the enlargement of Edo, the present Tōkyō, and the actual work was begun four years later. Edo castle was constructed towards the edge of high ground, and the soil cut from this site was used to fill alluvial swamp for the town site. In the centre was the 'Hommaru', the Central Rampart; to the east, the 'Ni-no-maru', or second rampart; and the San-no-maru, the third rampart; to the west, the 'Nishi-maru'; to the north the 'Hokkaku', to the far west the 'Fukiage' Rampart, and others to the south-east. All of these were arranged in a spiral stepped form, and the total area enclosed by these ramparts and the sea was about 320 acres. The castle town faced the sea to the south-west with a beach villa, called the Ōhama Goten, in its southern corner, intended to function as a detached fort. Enclosed by the central rampart was the private residence of the 'Shōgun', the government officers' quarters, and the keep. According to an estimate made in 1945, the total building area of this section, with the exception of the keep, was about $4/5$ acre. Within the first West Rampart was the residence for the 'Shōgun''s son, and the Momijiyama Hill, where the mausoleums of the 'Shōguns' were later constructed. Within the Fukiage Rampart were the residences and magnificent gardens for the members of the Tokugawa family. Within the Northern Rampart were the residences for the higher vassals. Other ramparts enclosed residences for the highest officers of the government, and beyond was the area for the residences of the feudal lords who were obliged to live in Edo each alternate year.

All the peripheral suburbs of the town were ruled directly by the 'Shōgun', who installed many low ranking 'samurai' in these areas. These were the usual arrangements of military forces in the battlefield during the mediaeval wars, with the lord in the centre surrounded by warriors in decreasing order of rank. Thus peacetime Edo was planned on a wartime basis. This type of spatial disposition was a formal representation of the feudal structure of centralism, and was entirely different from the form of the ancient capitals.

In 1657, on the 18th and 19th of January, 102,000 people died in a fire in Edo which destroyed the area inside the Central Rampart of the castle; 500 residences of the feudal lords, 770 residences of the vassals, 800 peripheral streets and bridges, more than 350 shrines and temples, and the citizens' houses in 400 'chō' streets were also destroyed. The original strategic form of the city was not rebuilt. The keep has never been reconstructed, and there was a large scale transfer of the residences to sites outside the castle. Those temples which had been in the central area were transferred to the periphery, the rivers were adjusted, redirected and controlled, and the marshes filled to make sites for new residences. The number of streets was augmented, from 930, in the beginning of the eighteenth century, to 1,679 by about the year 1830. Originally there had been only 300 streets in Edo. The expansion of the town, both in area and population, was stimulated by successive economic reconstruction after the many fires, which occurred so frequently there.

In the nineteenth century only 20% of the total area was allotted to the common citizenry, although they comprised 50% of the population. With the exception of the original commercial centre inside the Outer Rampart, the citizens' residences were dispersed among the warriors'. The warriors occupied 60% of the city area and the temples the remaining 20%.

The castle towns were a combination of two different quarters, each of different origin. One was the mediaeval fort and residential quarter for the feudal lord, his warriors, and craftsmen engaged in military production; the other was the mediaeval market town in the vicinity of the dwelling of the feudal lord. The warriors' quarters were compact, but the market town was linear. The castle town was the link between these two areas. The residence of the feudal lord, a symbolic tower keep, formed the pinnacle of the town. Surrounding the keep were the residences of the vassals, which were enclosed by the castle ditch. Outside the castle were dwellings of the warriors of high and low rank, and beyond the civilian quarter lived the merchant class.

At first the custom was followed of including the craftsmen's quarters inside the fort, when the castle towns were newly constructed, but with the end of the mediaeval wars the craftsmen gradually moved to the market quarter and found other work in the commercial district.

For defense purposes the main road linking the town to the surrounding country had many bends, running through the merchants' quarter and never through the centre of the town. The 'Tōkaidō' highway was bent no fewer than twenty-seven times in its passage through the town of Okazaki. The merchants' shops fronted onto the main road, and along the back lanes of the merchants' quarters were the craftsmen's houses. Beyond this again dwelt the warriors of the lowest class, and the servants. Within the warriors' quarters, also for defense purposes, there were few cross-streets, and most road junctions were T-shaped or L-shaped. Lastly the temples were arranged along the periphery and the whole surrounded by a ditch or moat.

This schematic description of the layout of a castle town was followed all over Japan, and was a spatial realization of the social structure which ensured the continuity of the Japanese feudal system. An act passed by the Tokugawa government made rank and profession hereditary, with the warriors as the highest rank, followed by the peasants who were forbidden to live in the castle towns, the craftsmen, and finally the merchants. This made it impossible for the castle towns to function as an organic whole. The towns were separated into two distinct and fixed areas with different patterns of everyday life: the productive, active merchants' and craftsmens' quarter, and the political, but otherwise unproductive, warriors' quarter, which was then merely a symbol of the power of the lord.

This dualistic organization was mirrored in the rural houses of petty landlords of the same period, where there was a production section of stores, kitchens, and living quarters, and a formal section for receiving guests. Its size indicated the wealth and the social status of the owner.

The merchant-craftsmens' quarter was simply inserted between the quarters for low- and high-class warriors, and subdivided into blocks, according to the nature of their trade or manufacture. In comparison with the ancient cities, the castle towns had a much more active life, but this irrational tendency to group similar functions together, instead of organizing the city as an organic whole, established the habits of modern urban life. In urban Japan today, for example, specific shops, groups of cinemas, and entertainment quarters are concentrated in separate areas.

The merchant class gradually became prosperous because of its commercial activity, in contrast with the destitute warrior class. With this increase of wealth and activity, the rigid zoning system began to disintegrate as the merchant class extended its district beyond the urban centre into the warriors' quarter, and the amorphous structure of the later castle town began to develop. From the beginning of the seventeenth century until the latter half of the eighteenth century the castle towns declined as commercial centres, while the commercial activity of ports and other rural towns grew apace.

The areas of the building lots of the warriors were graded according to their salaries – called 'kokudaka' – which were paid in grain.

At Nagaoka in 1621, the dwelling lots of the warrior were as follows:

Salary	Dimensions of lot	Area of lot
300–200 'koku'	25 'ken' by 25 'ken'	625 'tsubo'
200–100 'koku'	24 'ken' by 24 'ken'	576 'tsubo'
90– 50 'koku'	20 'ken' by 17 'ken'	340 'tsubo'
less than 40 'koku'	20 'ken' by 15 'ken'	300 'tsubo'
'Ashigaru': attendants		60 'tsubo'
'Chūgen': household servants		32 'tsubo'

Note: 1 'koku' = 4.96 bushels. 1 'ken' = 6 feet. 1 'tsubo' = 3.95 sq. yards. Note also that the 'tsubo' of the Edo Period is distinctly smaller than that of Heian-kyō.

The dimensions of their houses in 1658 were:

Salary	Length of beam span	Length of house
more than 200 'koku'	2–3.5 'ken'	less than 12 'ken'
less than 200 'koku'	2–3.5 'ken'	7–10 'ken'
'Kogumi': lower class	2–2.5 'ken'	5 'ken'
'Ashigaru': attendants	2 'ken'	5 'ken'
'Chūgen': household servants	1.5 'ken'	4 'ken'

The building lots of merchants and craftsmen were usually 15 'ken'–20 'ken' by about 5–6 'ken' (30–40 yards × 10–12 yards). This basic unit could be doubled or halved according to their wealth and social standing.

The width of the main roads passing through the town were 4–6 'ken' (8–12 yards), and the other roads in the town 2–4 'ken' (4–8 yards). The main roads running through the merchants' quarters were closed at night with wooden rail gates.

The streets of the warriors' quarter were named according to the specific roles of their residents, for example, 'Okachi-machi', infantrymen's street, 'Dō-shin-machi', policeman's street, 'Kosho-machi', boy warriors' street, 'Teppō-machi', gunmen's street. Sometimes they were named 'Sengoku machi', 1,000 'koku' of rice, and 'Hyakukoku-machi', 100 'koku' of rice, according to their salaries, and sometimes they were called 'Genba-machi' and 'Kazue-machi', according to their official ranks.

The streets in the craftsmen's quarter were named after the occupations of their inhabitants, such as 'Kajiya-machi', smiths' street, 'Konya-machi', dyers' street, 'Daiku-machi' or 'Bancho-machi', carpenters' street, 'Saiku-machi', cabinet makers' street, 'Himonoshi-machi', wood workers' street, 'Togiya-machi', sword grinders' street, 'Takumi-machi', craftsmen's street, 'Oga-machi', timber cutters' street, 'Tatami-machi', 'tatami'-mat makers' street, 'Imoji-machi', casters' street, and 'Shokunin-machi', workers' street, etc. At first these quarters were assigned to groups of craftsmen who gave their names to the streets, among which the names of smith, dyer and carpenter occurred most frequently. However they were never solely occupied by craftsmen of any one kind.

The streets of the merchants' quarter were named according to their trades, or the merchandise sold, such as 'Ryōgae-machi', bankers' street, 'Gofuku-machi', clothiers' street, 'Zaimoku-machi', timber merchants' street, 'Cha-machi', tea merchants' street, 'Kamiya-machi', paper merchants' street, 'Komeya-machi', rice merchants' street, 'Shio-machi', salt merchants' street, 'Uo-machi', fishmongers' street, etc. The 'Shio-machi' for salt merchants was situated at one end of the town beside the 'Tenma-machi', horses for hire, and the 'Uo-machi' for fishmongers was situated along a back lane because of their smell. Besides these, some streets were named according to their size or relative location, as 'Hon-machi', middle street, and 'Shita-machi', lower street.

Some merchants were wealthy and ran stores belonging to the feudal government, while others had privately owned stalls along the streets. Temporary markets, called 'sansai-ichi', if held three days each month, and 'rokusai-ichi', if held six days each month, were periodically moved to different towns or sites in the town. At annual festivals of shrines and temples provisional markets were opened around the temples for several days, and the wares spread out on straw mats on either side of the street.

The numbers of houses classified according to their occupations, as recorded in an early eighteenth century census of the Akashi castle town were as follows:

Occupation	Number of houses inside the Town	Number of houses outside the Town
Doctor, including surgeons and oculists	about 25 houses	about 75 houses
Carpenter	100 houses	150 houses
Pharmacist	6 houses	
Roofer	16 houses	
Plasterer	10 houses	
Shipbuilder	14 houses	4 houses
Woodworker	14 houses	
Smith	47 houses	
Cooper	53 houses	20 houses
Rice merchant	100 houses	
Dried-sardine fertilizer merchant	50 houses	
Oil merchant	41 houses	
Soy sauce merchant	3 houses	
Vinegar merchant	2 houses	
Pawnbroker	41 houses	
Wholesalers, and misc.	54 houses	
Lumber yards	about 3 houses	
Fishmonger	56 houses	
	and 5 wholesale fish shops	
Greengrocer	about 8 houses	
Fancy goods store	80 houses	
Dying shop	39 houses	about 3 houses
'Tatami'-mat shop	11 houses	
Draper	11 houses	
Second-hand clothes		
Tailor	2 houses	
Roof-tile maker	2 houses	16 houses
Hair-dresser	24 persons	
Inn	27 houses	
Wine shop	15 houses	

Although Akashi was a local port as well as a castle town, this table serves to illustrate the everyday life in the castle towns of that time.

The population of the castle towns, excluding the warriors and their servants, and the ratio of the population of the town with that of the whole feudal territorial province were:

Town	Population	Ratio	Date
Kanazawa	55,506 persons	9.6%	1644
Kanazawa	55,101 persons	9.5%	1667
Kanazawa	56,355 persons	n.a.	1810
Okayama	28,298 persons	7.7%	1707
Himeji	22,390 persons	n.a.	1740
Hiroshima	31,207 persons	n.a.	1677
Tokushima	20,590 persons	n.a.	1685
Sasayama	2,673 persons	n.a.	1760

Matsumoto	8,278 persons	7.6%	1722
Matsumoto	8,073 persons	n.a.	1723

In Matsumoto in 1725, there are recorded 1,233 commoner families, 2,315 households, and 8,206 persons, 4,317 men and 3,889 women. The warrior population totalled 6,191 persons: upper class 2,229, itemized as 580 men, 538 women, 555 men-servants and 566 woman-servants; middle class 1519 persons, as 659 men, 717 women, 43 men-servants, 100 women-servants; lower class 2,324 persons, as 1,363 men, 961 women; and 110 retired warriors and their assistants. Besides these people 1300 warriors, and their attendants, from Matsumoto, were living in Edo, making the total population about 14,000 people. The population in the Matsumoto feudal district, which included 259 villages, was 82,139 in 1783. The rice crop was 60,000 'koku' according to the official register, but was actually probably about 88,000 'koku'.

The 261 feudal districts throughout Japan were abolished in 1871, in the fourth year of the Meiji Era, and the prefectural system of the Imperial government was readopted. Three special districts around the three most important cities of Tōkyō, Ōsaka, and Kyōto, and 302 prefectures, were at first drawn up, but were later reorganized into three special districts and 73 prefectures. Most local seats of government were located in the former castle towns.

Of the 64 newly instituted local government towns in the Meiji Era, 46 were former castle towns. Of the 452 former castle towns 113 were legalized as cities, and 174 (38%) as towns, a total of 63%. Thus it can be said that more than 60% of modern Japanese cities are descended from the end of the Middle Ages, with their origins in these former castle towns.

The Port Town

Of the towns situated along the main traffic routes, those on the sea routes – the ports – developed most strikingly. The prosperity of the port towns was caused by the increase in variety and quantity of local production of goods such as 'sake', cotton, dried sardines for fertilizer, and textiles, and their resulting wide distribution throughout Japan. Sea routes were established both to the east and west of Honshū

in the seventeenth century, and many ports developed along the coasts of the Japanese islands, especially along the Inland Sea, which had been the main sea route since ancient times. Among the most prosperous towns were Ōsaka, Hyōgo, the present Kōbe, Onomichi, and Akamaseki, the present Shimonoseki, in the west. Onomichi was called Ko-edo, which meant small Edo, and in 1801 had five or six thousand houses. The streetscape was probably very similar to that of Edo, with many two-story tile-roofed houses. In the port towns there were new establishments concerned with the distribution of goods, for example warehouses, inns, wholesale shops and pawn shops, as well as the merchants of other cities.

The social and spatial organization of the ports is typified by Sakai.

In ancient times, Sakai was a fisherman's village on the border of the Settsu and Izumi districts. By the middle of the Kamakura Period it was separated into two parts: Hoku-sho, the northern quarter and Nansho, the southern quarter, divided by the central Ōshoji Street on the borderline of the two districts.

In the Nanbokuchō Period, in the middle of the fourteenth century, when the Southern and Northern emperors were fighting, Sakai played an important role in the war as a naval and military base of the armies and navies of Shikoku and Kyūshū. Sakai was several times a battlefield as the opposing sides fought to occupy the city, and at the end of the war was controlled by the Asikaga group. Under the Ashikaga's Muromachi government the control of the city passed into the hands of the Yamana family, and then the Ōuchi family. This family was the strongest clan in the Inland Sea and ruled Sakai until the end of the Middle Ages.

In 1399, Ashikaga Yoshimitsu assaulted Sakai when the Ouchi army rebelled against the 'Shōgun'. The Ōuchi family constructed a rampart about one mile square enclosing the city, and made use of the southeastern swamp as a barricade. They built 98 observatories and 1,125 keeps. All the inhabitants of Sakai, both the 5,000 warriors and all the citizens, were besieged until a terrible fire burnt the whole town of 10,000 houses.

Sakai rebelled again in the Ōnin Era, in 1476, for

ten years, and was a battlefield for the warring factions of the East and West armies until 1482. During this time, the Hosokawa family of the East Army occupied Sakai and used it as a military base against Hyōgo, which was used as a base by the West. The Hosokawa family perfected the port of Sakai, and after the end of the war the town prospered, and was designated as the terminal of the sea traffic between Ming China and Japan.

Periodical markets had been held in Sakai since the fourteenth century, and commercial guilds were established for the sale of hats, horses, fish, and salted vegetables. Textile manufacture improved with the skills of workers from Yamaguchi, who were influenced by Chinese techniques, and with workers from the government atelier in Kyōto. Many utensils coated with lacquer, called 'urushi', were made, and metal workers were established. All these trades prospered. Many temples in Nara and Kōyasan, which had been large landowners from ancient times, used Sakai as the port for their rice crops; timber was imported from Awa, in Shikoku, and salt from the Inland Sea. Warehouses, wholesale stores, money lenders and pawnbrokers were established and merchants traded with Ming China, Korea, and Ryūkyū, the present Okinawa. The vast profits which accumulated from this commercial activity caused the merchants to employ wandering warriors to guard the town from hostile feudal lords.

Both Luis Frais' 'History of Japan' of 1599 and Fr. Gaspard Vilela's diary of 1562 give descriptions of Sakai. The west side faced the sea, and the other three sides were enclosed by moats. The two gates of the town were kept closed and locked, protecting both travellers and inhabitants of the town as if in a castle. The population was calculated to be about 20,000 people in the first half of the sixteenth century, but it had grown to 63,000 by 1695.

The municipal government was managed by the 'egoshu' council without regulation by feudal lords. This autonomous organization was followed by other port towns such as Ōminato in Ise, Akita in Dewa, Tsuruga in Echizen, and Hakata in Kyūshū which modeled their governments on Sakai.

When Toyotomi Hideyoshi constructed his magnif-

icent castle town of Ōsaka he compelled merchants from Sakai and other cities to transfer there, and filled in the canals of Sakai in the 1580's. This was fatal not only for the prosperity of Sakai but also for the growth of the autonomous city in Japan. The wealth of Sakai was moved to Ōsaka under the control of Hideyoshi.

With the establishment of a regular sea route between Ōsaka and Edo in the latter half of the seventeenth century, merchant ships, called 'hishigaki-kaisen', which had been designed by the merchants of Sakai, terminated their voyages at Ōsaka instead of Sakai. As a result common everyday goods such as cotton, oil, 'sake', vinegar, and soy sauce, and even goods produced locally, now only rarely passed through Sakai.

When construction work changed the course of the Yamato River and its estuary from Ōsaka to Sakai in 1704, the history of the town as a port gradually declined. Silt deposited by the river on the sea bed made it necessary to construct piers to guard the harbor, thus making it difficult for ships to enter and leave the port. Sakai changed from a port town to an inland town.

The plan of Sakai was divided into two by the border between the Settsu and Izumi districts; the southern quarter was a rectangle and the northern quarter was a parallelogram. Both were divided into rectangular blocks, by a grid of streets. The peripheral canal, and the sea, as well as the flat southeastern swamp topography, constituted a defense similar to the recent castle towns, but inside the town there was no central focus such as the keep of the castle town or the Imperial court of the ancient capitals, and no hierarchical zoning, or symbols of authority. These characteristics of the urban plan of Sakai might have been the foundation for the growth of a free, equal and democratic society. However, the emerging democracy could not survive as the people of Sakai had neither armies nor control over the surrounding farmland, as did the feudal lords, but had to depend on the power of wealth and the organized unity of the citizens to sustain their way of life.

Chronological Table

Dates	Periods	Emperors		Capitals
300	Jōmon (about 4500 B.C.–250 B.C.)			
200	Yayoi (200 B.C.–250 A.D.)			
	v			
100	v	Sujin-tennō (97–30 B.C.)		
	v			
200	v			
	Kofun (250–552)			
300	v			
	v			
400	v			
	v			
500	v			
	Asuka (552–645)			
600	v	Suiko-tennō (592–628)		
	Hakuhō (645–710)			
	v			
	v			
	v	Temmu-tennō (673–686)		
	v			
700	Nara (710–794)	Gemmyō-tennō (707–715)	710	Heijō-kyō (Nara)
	v			
	v	Shōmu-tennō (724–749)		
	v			
	v			
	v			
	v			
	v	Kammu-tennō (781–806)		
800	Heian (794–1185)		794	Heian-kyō (Kyoto)
	v			
	v			
900	v			
	v			
1000	v			
	v	Shirakawa-tennō (1072–1086)		
1100	v	from 1086 'insei'-Regency		
	v			
	v			
	v			
	Kamakura (1185–1392)			
1200	v			
	v			
	v			
	v			

Monuments		Events and famous persons
		Cord-marking ceramic and 'dogū'-figures
		'dōtaku' bronze bells
		'haniwa'
	300–710	Yamato government, Clans' system ('uji')
	Burial Mound	
		558 Introduction of Buddhism
588	Asuka-dera	574–622 Shōtoku-taishi Regent
607	Hōryū-ji (finished 746)	
		645–649 Taika reform
685	Ise Shrine (rebuilt every twenty years)	
710	Kōfuku-ji	701 Taihō edict
717	Yakushi-ji	712 Writing of the 'Kojiki'
	Izumo Shrine (eldest Shrine, today's building	720 Writing of the 'Nihon-Shoki'
	of the middle of the 18th century)	741 Buddhism state religion
About 730	Tōdai-ji	Building of the main provincial shrines
759	Tōshōdai-ji	('kokubun-ji')
	Murō-ji, founded at the end of the 8th century	759 Achievement of the Manyō-shū
	(Kondō and Pagoda from the 9th century)	
		774–835 Kūkai, founder of the Shingon school
		Expansion of the japanese vowel-writing
859	Iwashimizu-Hachiman-gū	
874	Daigo-ji	
947	Kitano Shrine	942–1017 Eshin diffuses the Jōdo doctrine
1053	Byōdō-in Hōō-dō	
	Jōruri-ji, late Heian	1133–1212 Hōnen Shōnin founds 1175 the Jōdo school
1108	Konjiki-dō in Chūson-ji	1147–1199 Minamoto Yoritomo, first 'shōgun' in 1192
		Military regime in Kamakura
1160	Shiramizu-Amida-dō	1173–1262 Shinran Shōnin founds the Jōdo-shinshū
1164	Sanjūsangen-dō (today's building from 1251)	
1202	Kennin-ji	1200–1253 Dōgen Zenshi preaches the Zen doctrine
1239	Tōfuku-ji	1222–1282 Nichiren, founder of the Hokke-shū
1244	Eihei-ji	
1253	Kenchō-ji	

Dates	Periods	Emperors	Capitals
	Kamakura (1185–1392)		
	v		
	v	Go-Daigo-tennō (1318–1339)	
1300	v		
	v		
	v		
1400	Muromachi or Ashikaga (1392–1573)		
	v		
	v		
	v		
1500	v		
	v		
	v		
	v		
	Momoyama (1573–1603)		1603 Edo (Capital of the Shōgunat)
	v		
	v		
1600	Tokugawa or Edo (1603–1868)		
	v		
	v		
	v		
	v		
	v		
	v		
1700	v		
	v	Meiji-tennō (1866(1868)–1912)	1869 Tōkyō
1800	v		
	v		
1900	v		

Monuments	Events and famous persons

1282	Enkaku-ji	1274–1281	Raid of the Mongols in Kyūshū
1324	Daitoku-ji	1275–1351	Musō Soseki, priest of the Zen Rinzai sect
1338	Myōshin-ji		
		1358–1408	Ashikaga Yoshimitsu, 'shōgun'
1450	Ryōan-ji	1420–1506	Zeami, founder of the Nō
		1467–1477	Ōnin rebellion
1483	Ginkaku-ji	1521–1591	Sen no Rikyū, Teamaster
1513	Hondō from Daisen-in in Daitoku-ji	1534–1582	Oda Nobunaga unified the country
		1542–1616	Tokugawa Ieyasu, statesman
		1549	Francis Xavier, missionary in Japan
1579	Azuchi Castle	1579–1647	Kobori Enshū, Teamaster
1580	Himeji Castle	1590	Hideyoshi ends the pacification of the Empire
1584	Ōsaka Castle	1592–1595	Hideyoshi's first campaign against Corea
1590	Katsura-rikyū	1603	Ieyasu founder of the Shōgunat's government in Edo
1594	Nishi-Hongan-ji-shoin		
1602	Nijō Castle	1615	Destruction of the main castles
1636	Tōshōgū Shrine in Nikkō	1617	Establishment of the prostitution's quarter of Yoshiwara in Edo
		1657	Burning of Edo
1675	Mampuku-ji		
		1858	Conclusion of trade-agreements
		1862	Embassy to Europe
		1867	The end of the Tokugawa government
		1868	Reinstalment of the Emperor. Reforms. Beginning of the industrial development

Bibliography

TASJ: Transactions of the Asiatic Society of Japan

Alex, W.
Architektur der Japaner. Ravensburg, 1965

Altherr, A.
Three Japanese Architects – Drei japanische Architekten
(Mayekawa, Tange, Sakakura). Stuttgart, 1968

Baltzer, F.
Die Architektur der Kultbauten Japans. Berlin, 1907

Blaser, W.
Japanese Temples and Tea Houses. New York, 1956

Blaser, W.
Wohnen und Bauen in Japan. Teufen, 1958

Blaser, W.
Struktur und Gestalt in Japan. Zurich, 1963

Carver, N. F.
Form and Space of Japanese Architecture. Tokyo, 1955

Cram, R. A.
Impressions of Japanese Architecture and the
Allied Arts. 1930

Drexler, A.
The Architecture of Japan. New York, 1955

Engel, H.
Japanese Gardens for Today. Rutland (Vermont), 1959

Engel, H.
The Japanese House – A Tradition for Contemporary
Architecture. Rutland (Vermont), 1964

Fujioka, M.
Sumiya. Tokyo, 1957

Futagawa, Y., Itō, T.
The Roots of Japanese Architecture. London, 1964

Futagawa, Y.
The Essential Japanese House. Tokyo, New York, 1967

Gropius, W., Ishimoto, Y., Tange, K.
Katsura – Tradition and Creation in Japanese
Architecture. New Haven, 1960

Guillain, F.
Châteaux-Forts Japonais. 1942

Hisamatsu, S.
Zen and Fine Arts (Zen to Bijutsu). Kyōto, 1958

Horiguchi,
The Katsura Imperial Villa. 1953

Iwamiya, T., Richie, D.
Japon, Beauté des Formes. Fribourg, 1964

Iwamiya, T., Richie, D.
Le Japon des Formes. Fribourg, 1965

Karow, O., Seckel, D.
Der Ursprung des Torii, in 'Mitteilungen der Deutschen
Gesellschaft für Natur und Völkerkunde Ostasiens'. 1942

Kishida, H.
Japanese architecture. Tokyo, Tourist Library, Japanese
Government Railways. 1935

Kirby, J. B.
From castle to teahouse. Japanese architecture of the
Momoyama period. Rutland (Vermont), 1962

Kitao, H.
Shoin Architecture (Shoin Kenchiku). 1953

Kitao, H.
Chanoyu Houses (Sukiya). 1953

Kojiro, Y., Futagawa, Y.
Forms in Japan. Honolulu, 1965

Kultermann, U.
Neues Bauen in Japan. Tübingen, 1960

Kümmel, O.
Die Kunst Chinas, Japans und Koreas ('Handbuch der
Kunstwissenschaft'). Wildpark-Potsdam, 1929

Mac Clatchie, Th.R.H.
'The Castle of Yedo', in: TASJ, vol. 6, pt. I, pp. 119–150

Mac Clatchie, Th.R.H.
'The Feudal Mansions of Yedo', in: TASJ, vol. 7, pt. III, pp. 157–186

Mecking, L.
Japanische Stadtlandschaften. 1930

Mecking, L.
Japans Häfen, in 'Mitteilungen der Geographischen Gesellschaft', Hamburg, XLII, 1931

Mogi, H.
A Historical Study of the Development of Edo 1660–1860. Tokyo, 1966

Mori, O.
Katsura Villa. 1930

Morse, E.S.
Japanese Homes and their Surroundings. Vienna, 1885

Nishihara, K.
Japanese Houses, Patterns for Living. Tokyo, 1968

Noma, S.
The Arts of Japan, Ancient and Medieval. Tokyo, 1965

Noma, S.
The Arts of Japan, Late Medieval to Modern. Tokyo, 1967

Ooka, M., Mori, O.
Pageant of Japanese Art, Bd. 6, Tokyo, 1954

Ooka, M., Mori, O.
History of Japanese Architecture and Gardens. Tokyo, 1957

Ota, H. (ed.).
Japanese Architecture and Gardens. Tokyo, The Society for International Cultural Relations. 1966

Paine, P.T., Soper, A.C.
Art and Architecture of Japan. Harmondsworth, 1955–1960 (Pelican History of Art)

Perkins, P.O.
The Rise and Decline of Bukezukuri, in 'Monumenta Nipponica', vol. II, pp. 596–608

Ponsonby-Fane, R.A.B.
Ancient Capitals and Palaces of Japan, in 'Transactions of the Japan Society of London', vol. XX, 1922–1923

Studies in Shinto and Shrines. Ponsonby-Fane series, vol. I, Kyōto, 1954

Kyōto, the Old Capital of Japan. Ponsonby-Fane series, vol. II, Kyōto, 1956

Misasagi: The Imperial Mausolea of Japan. Ponsonby-Fane series, vol. III, Kyōto, 1959

Visiting Famous Shrines in Japan. Ponsonby-Fane series, vol. VI, Kyōto, 1964

Sadler, A.L.
A short History of Japanese Architecture. Sidney/London, 1941

Sadler, A.L.
Cha-no-Yu: The Japanese Tea Ceremony. Rutland (Vermont), 1963 (1st Edition 1933)

Sansom, G.B.
Japan, a Short Cultural History. New York, 1943

Sansom, G.B.
A History of Japan. London, 1958

Satow, E.
'The Shinto Temples of Ise', in: TASJ, vol. 2, 1874

Seckel, D.
Taigenkyū, das Heiligtum des Yiitsu-Shintō, in 'Monumenta Nipponica', vol. VI, Tokyo, 1943

Seckel, D.
Buddhistische Kunst Ostasiens. Stuttgart, 1957

Seckel, D.
Einführung in die Kunst Ostasiens. Munich, 1960

Seckel, D.
Kunst des Buddhismus. Baden-Baden, 1962

Scheid, L.
Die Kulturlandschaft Alt-Japans. Tokyo, 1937

Schwarz, W.L.
'The Great Shrine of Izumo, Some notes on Shinto,
Ancient and Modern', in: TASJ, vol. 41, pt. IV, Tokyo, 1913

Sen, S., Murata, J., Kitamura, D.
Cashitsu: The Original Drawings and Photographic
Illustrations of the Typical Japanese Tea Architecture and
dens. Tokyo, 1959

Tange, K., Kawazoe, N., Watanabe, Y.
Ise, prototype of Japanese architecture. Cambridge, Mass.,
M.I.T. Press 1965

Taut, B.
Houses and People of Japan. Tokyo, 1958

Trewartha, G.T.
'Japanese Cities: Distribution and Morphology', in:
Geographical Review, vol. 24, pp. 404–417

Trewartha, G.T.
Japan, a Physical, Cultural and Regional Geography. 1945

Yamata, J.
The Shōji, Japanese Interiors and Silhouettes. 1929

Yoshida, T.
Das Japanische Wohnhaus. Tübingen, 1935/1954

Yoshida, T.
Japanische Architektur. Tübingen, 1952